# Science for All Seasons
# Spring

## Grades PreK-K

**Project Manager:**
Allison E. Ward

**Writers:**
Lucia Kemp Henry
Dr. Suzanne Moore

**Contributing Editors:**
Cindy K. Daoust, Ada Goren, Sherri Lynn Kuntz

**Art Coordinator:**
Kimberly Richard

**Artists:**
Pam Crane, Theresa Lewis Goode, Sheila Krill, Mary Lester,
Kimberly Richard, Greg D. Rieves,
Rebecca Saunders, Barry Slate

**Cover Artist:**
Kimberly Richard

www.themailbox.com

©2000 by THE EDUCATION CENTER, INC.
All rights reserved.
ISBN #1-56234-383-1

Manufactured in the United States

10 9 8 7 6 5 4 3 2 1

# Table of Contents

# The World of Weather

## Investigating Rain

It's raining, it's pouring...and scientific knowledge will be soaring when you invite your students to spend some time investigating rain!

### Who Likes Rain?

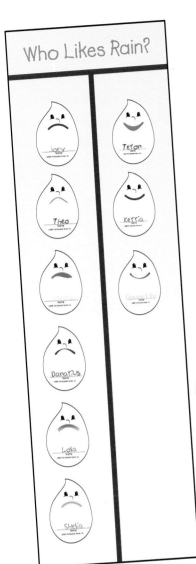

How many of your little ones delight in the sight of a rainy-day downpour? Find out with this graphing activity. To prepare, create a two-column graph labeled as shown. Then ask your youngsters if they like or dislike rain. After discussing students' feelings, give each child a photocopied raindrop pattern from page 8. If the child likes rain, have her draw a smile on her raindrop. If she does not like rain, have her draw a frown. Ask each child to write her name on the line, cut out her raindrop, and post it on the graph. Then take a few minutes to discuss the results. Once you've completed the activities in this unit, poll students and graph their attitudes a second time. You may find that those who once found rain to be a pain have changed their minds!

### Simulating Rain

Even if the forecast is for clear skies with not a shower in sight, your youngsters can simulate a rainstorm right inside the classroom! To begin this rhythmic rain simulation, have students sit cross-legged on the floor in a circle. Recite each stanza of the following chant, prompting students to perform the accompanying motion. Recite the first stanza in a whisper; then gradually increase the volume of your voice with each stanza. To finish off the faux rain shower, repeat the chant and sounds for each stanza in reverse order. There's nothing like the rhythmical sounds of a rainy day!

1. Rain, rain, rain, rain,
   Whispering on the windowpane.
   (Rub hands together.)

2. Rain, rain, rain, rain,
   Tapping on the windowpane.
   (Snap fingers.)

3. Rain, rain, rain, rain,
   Slapping on the windowpane.
   (Slap thighs with hands.)

4. Rain, rain, rain, rain,
   Drumming on the windowpane.
   (Slap floor with hands.)

## Let's Make Rain Sticks!

Introduce your youngsters to another way to simulate the sound of rain when you make rain sticks together in a small-group setting. To make a rain stick, first push 14 large (1½-inch) metal brads into a paper towel tube to form a random pattern along the entire length of the tube. Use tape to secure a cardboard circle (1½ inches in diameter) to one end of the tube. Next, place two to three tablespoons of *one* of the materials from the list below inside the tube. Then use more tape to secure another cardboard circle to the open end of the tube. Finish the rain stick by wrapping the tube with gift wrap or construction paper.

To use the rain stick, grasp each end lightly and hold the tube perpendicular to the floor. When you hear that all the material inside has "rained" to the lower end of the tube, flip the rain stick and begin the shower of sound all over again!

**Rain Stick Fillers**

| | | | |
|---|---|---|---|
| Rice Krispies® cereal | dried beans or peas | elbow macaroni | sequins |
| Cheerios® cereal | small metal washers | small plastic beads | aquarium |
| gravel | | | |

## Rain Stick Pairs

Each of the rain sticks your youngsters create for the previous activity will have its own unique sound, because of the variety of fillers and the differences in the brad patterns. Make some extra rain sticks with similar brad patterns and matching materials to test your youngsters' auditory skills. Use the directions in "Let's Make Rain Sticks!" to prepare two rain sticks with elbow macaroni, two with aquarium gravel, two with Rice Krispies® cereal, and two with sequins. Then gather a small group of students and invite them to play with the rain sticks for a few minutes. Encourage them to discuss the sounds they hear. Then challenge them to pair up the rain sticks that have the same sounds. After some trial and error and a bit of discussion, your little sound scientists should be able to make matches that are as right as rain!

## Sounds Like a Center

For a follow-up to the activity described in "Rain Stick Pairs," place the extra rain sticks you created in a center. Add four small zippered plastic bags, each containing one of the four fillers you used in the rain sticks. A youngster at this center matches the rain sticks that have similar sounds. Then he tries to determine which filler each rain stick pair contains. If desired, use sticky dots to color-code the rain sticks and plastic bags for self-checking.

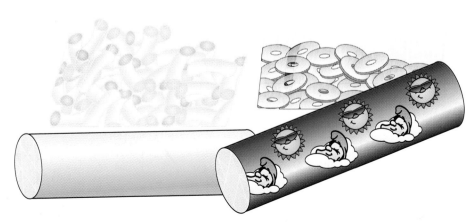

## Rain Indications

How can you tell that it's rained even if you haven't seen the rain falling? Pursue this question by asking students to imagine they have gone to bed one evening while the skies are clear. Upon awakening in the morning, what would they see outside to tell them that it had rained during the night? Encourage a discussion; then write your youngsters' ideas on chart paper. Later, use the students' suggestions in the song below.

### How Can You Tell It Has Rained?

The streets are wet.
The grass is wet.
You see puddles.
The slide is wet.
There are raindrops on the window.

## The Rain Came Down

Teach your young scientists this splashy song to the tune of "Buffalo Gals" to reinforce the ideas discussed in "Rain Indications" (above). Sing this song on a rainy spring day; then go outside for a postrain puddle hunt!

How do we know that it rained in the night,
Rained in the night, rained in the night?
How do we know that it rained in the night?
We see [that the streets are wet]!

*Substitute other student suggestions from the chart for the underlined phrase.*

## The Disappearing Puddle

Have your youngsters noticed that—little by little—even the biggest rain puddles eventually disappear? Here's an easy way to visually record the shrinkage of a puddle. To begin, take your class outdoors in the morning after a rain. Work together to find a big puddle on a paved surface. Use chalk to draw a line on the pavement just outside the perimeter of the puddle. Return to the puddle periodically to draw a new line around it. (Depending on the weather and the location of your puddle, you may need to return every hour or over the course of a day or two.) Encourage students to compare the old and new lines. Has the puddle changed in size? Continue to record the puddle's size until it disappears. Then talk about what has happened to the water. Share the information in "This Is Why" (at right) with your young puddle experts!

### This Is Why

When water puddles on a surface like a sidewalk or pavement, the heat of the sun slowly causes the liquid water to change into *water vapor,* which is a gas. The water vapor then rises into the air. This process is called *evaporation.* Water evaporates slowly, so the puddle shrinks over time.

## This Is Why

The more *absorbent* the surface, the shorter the "life span" of the puddle. Puddles disappear quickly on absorbent surfaces such as soil and sand, because the water simply soaks in.

## Which Puddle Persists?

How can you come up with puddles to study when there's not a rain shower in sight? Make some yourself! Prior to this activity, find areas outdoors suitable for making several puddles. You'll need to find a spot in the dirt, in the sand, on the grass, on a sidewalk, and on blacktop, if possible. Try to find five locations fairly close together. Next, prepare a chart with a column for each area where you plan to place a puddle.

Take your youngsters outdoors. Have student volunteers pour buckets of water on each of your five selected surfaces to create five puddles. (Pour an equal amount of water on each surface.) Once the puddles are made, ask students to predict which puddle of water will last the longest. To record the "life span" of each puddle, have students check them periodically (depending upon your weather). Record students' findings on the chart. Which puddle is the most persistent?

| time | sand | dirt | blacktop | sidewalk | grass |
|---|---|---|---|---|---|
| 10:00 | The puddle is gone already. | This puddle is much smaller. | This is the biggest puddle. | This puddle is still big. | This puddle is almost gone. |
| 11:30 | | This puddle is gone now. | This puddle got smaller. | This puddle is smaller. | This puddle is gone now. |
| 1:00 | | | This puddle got a little smaller. | This one is almost gone. | |
| 2:00 | | | Still here! | There's just a tiny bit left! | |

## Puddle Comparisons

Explore puddles further with this small-group activity at your sand table. Direct students to dig two depressions in the sand to create small basins for puddles. Lay a paper towel inside one basin; lay a piece of plastic wrap inside the other. Pour some water into each basin to make a puddle, being sure to keep the water level below the edge of the liner. Have students observe the puddles and describe what happens. Why do they think the puddle lined with the paper towel disappeared? Where did the water go?

Extend this absorbing experiment by inviting students to test other materials as puddle liners, such as waxed paper, muslin, a plastic bag, aluminum foil, and newsprint. Add a chart labeled as shown to the area. Have students cut and glue samples of the puddle-lining materials to the chart to display their findings.

## This Is Why

The puddle lined with plastic wrap lasts longer because the plastic wrap blocks the absorption of the water into the sand. The paper towel absorbs the water and allows it to soak into the sand quickly.

## Rain Gets Things Wet

Invite your weather-savvy students to create these rain-themed booklets. To prepare, duplicate the booklet cover and pages on pages 9–11 on white paper for each child. Read through the directions below and gather the necessary materials. (For younger students, you may wish to precut the circles on page 5 of the booklet.) Have each child cut out his cover and pages before illustrating them as directed below. Help each child complete his booklet by stacking the cover and pages in order and stapling them together along the left side.

**Cover:** Color the cloud gray. Glue blue paper strips to the bottom of the cloud to resemble rain. Write your name on the line.

**Page 1:** Color the windowpanes gray. Make dots on each pane with blue glitter glue.

**Page 2:** Color the cloud gray. Draw a house under the cloud. Glue pieces of blue yarn to the bottom of the cloud to resemble rain.

**Page 3:** Color the cloud gray. Draw green grass at the bottom of the page. Use a thin paintbrush to paint blue rain below the cloud.

**Page 4:** Color the cloud gray. Draw something that gets wet when it rains. Write the word on the blank. Use a blue marker to draw rain.

**Page 5:** Color the umbrella. Cut out the circle on the page. Tape a photocopy of your school photo to the back of the page so that your face shows through the opening. Use blue glitter glue to draw rain.

Rain Gets Things Wet
by Deidrick

©2000 The Education Center, Inc. • Science for All Seasons • Spring • TEC3049

Rain gets the window wet. 1.

Rain gets the house wet. 2.

Rain makes the grass wet. 3.

Rain gets the _____ wet. 4.

but it doesn't get me wet! 5.

## Home Learning Lab

Can you imagine how many times your youngsters' parents have searched for a way to entertain their little ones on a rainy day? Help them out by duplicating the "Home Learning Lab" on page 12 for each child. Then, when the forecast calls for a rainy weekend, send the list of activities home with each student. It's a sure bet that many parents will shower you with thanks!

## Singin' of the Rain

Reinforce the theme of the booklet with this song you *won't* want to save for a rainy day! To add additional verses, encourage students to suggest vocabulary from their "Rain Gets Things Wet" booklets to replace the underlined word.

*(sung to the tune of "If You're Happy and You Know It")*

Oh, do you know what happens when it rains? (clap, clap)
Oh, do you know what happens when it rains? (clap, clap)
When it rains, the [trees] get wet. Oh, yes! It's true, you bet!
Yes, that is just what happens when it rains! (clap, clap)

7

# Raindrop Patterns
Use with "Who Likes Rain?" on page 3.

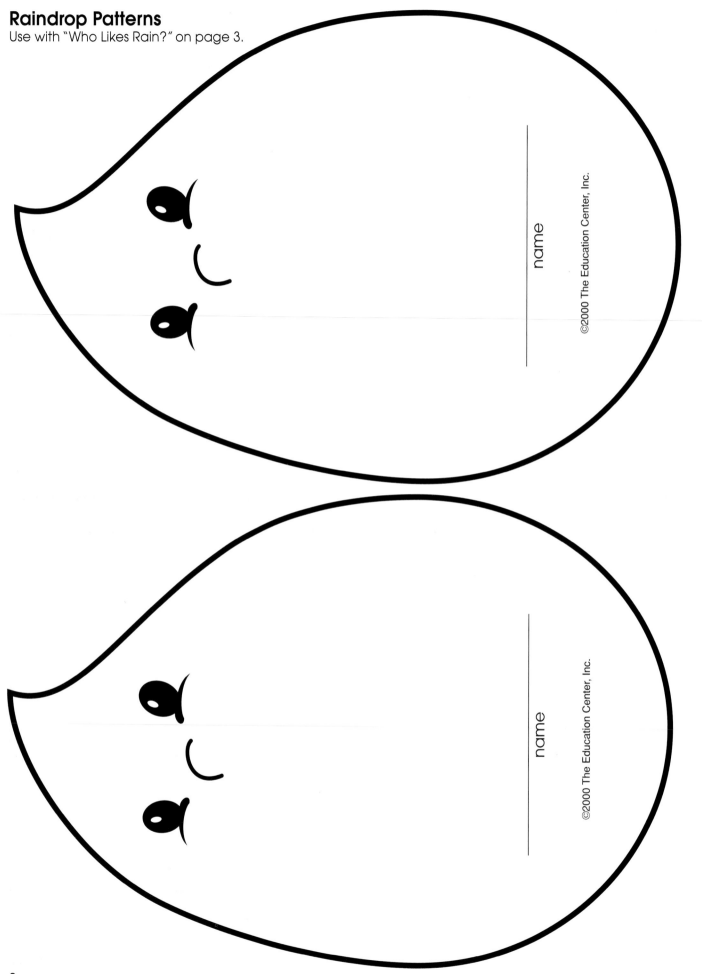

name

©2000 The Education Center, Inc.

name

©2000 The Education Center, Inc.

# Rain Gets Things Wet

by _____

Rain gets the window wet.

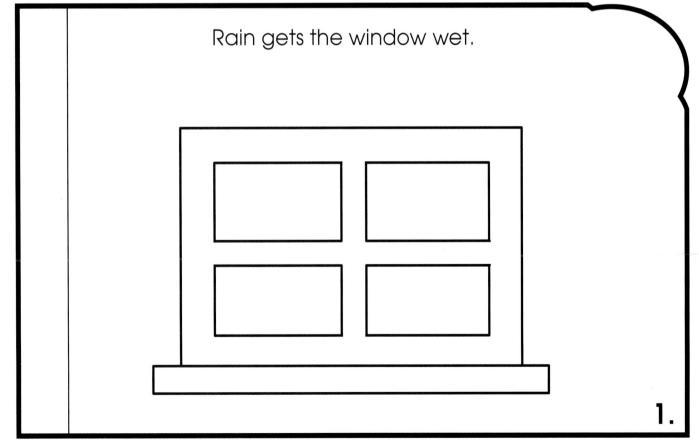

1.

## Booklet Pages 2 and 3
Use with "Rain Gets Things Wet" on page 7.

Rain gets the house wet.

2

Rain gets the grass wet.

3

Rain gets the _____ wet.

**4**

but it doesn't get me wet!

**5**

Dear Parents,

  We have been learning about rain at school. Here is a list of things to do at home on a rainy day. You and your child will have a great time investigating rain!

## Things to Do on a Rainy Day

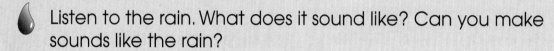 Listen to the rain. What does it sound like? Can you make sounds like the rain?

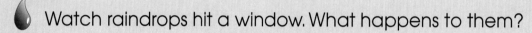 Watch raindrops hit a window. What happens to them?

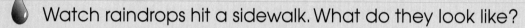 Watch raindrops hit a sidewalk. What do they look like?

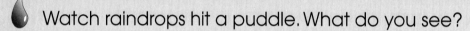 Watch raindrops hit a puddle. What do you see?

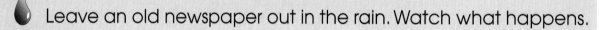 Leave an old newspaper out in the rain. Watch what happens.

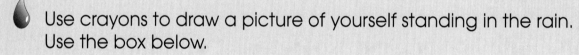 Use crayons to draw a picture of yourself standing in the rain. Use the box below.

©2000 The Education Center, Inc. • *Science for All Seasons* • *Spring* • TEC3049

# Little Sprouts

Your little ones will be sprouting up lots of scientific knowledge as they explore and discover what seeds, edible bulbs, flowering bulbs, and vegetable tops have in common!

## Interesting Edibles

Give your little ones a taste of fun as they investigate sprouts! To prepare, ask parents to donate different types of edible sprouts from your local grocery or health food store. Invite each child to put a spoonful of sprouts on a small paper plate; then have him examine his sprouts. Tell students that the sprouts before them are edible. After discussing student observations, encourage your youngsters to taste several sprouts. Mmmm, interesting!

## No Soil or Sunlight Needed!

Now that your little ones have observed sprouts, they will be eager to grow their own! Have parents donate alfalfa seeds, mustard seeds, or dried chickpeas from your local grocery or health food store. Put the seeds in a shallow pan of water and soak them overnight; then rinse the seeds in a colander. Have each student put a spoonful of seeds in a personalized clear plastic cup and then use a rubber band to secure a 5" x 5" muslin square to the top. Have students predict what will happen to the seeds without soil and sunlight. Then have students set their cups in a warm, dark place. Daily, remind each student to gently pour water through the muslin of her cup, swirl the seeds around in the water, and then pour the water out through the muslin. In approximately three days, your youngsters will be delighted to see that their seeds have sprouted without soil or sunlight. Vary this activity with lentils, mung beans, or cress seeds. Anyone for sprouts?

### This Is Why

Seeds can sprout, or germinate, without direct sunlight or nutrients from the soil because each seed has its own food that allows it to sprout and begin growing in moist, warm conditions.

## Cozy or Chilly?

Your youngsters will find out if seeds sprout in warm or cool temperatures with this scientific experiment. In advance, ask your local grocery store to donate two foam meat trays. Line each tray with a layer of wet cotton balls. Spread two tablespoons of alfalfa seeds evenly on each tray. Have your students predict how warm or cool temperatures will affect the seeds. Then place one tray in a sunny area and the other tray in a refrigerator. After several days, your students will notice that the seeds getting warmth from the sun are sprouting. Ask them to predict what the seeds in the refrigerator look like. Then have your little ones compare the trays. Seeds like it warm!

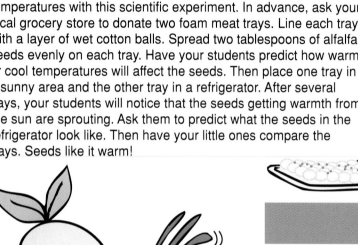

## Bunches of Bulbs

Reinforce observation skills with this small-group activity. To prepare, have parents donate edible bulbs, such as white onions, yellow onions, red onions, small pearl onions, green onions (scallions), garlic, and leeks. When all the bulbs have arrived, put them on a table and invite each student in a small group to observe and compare the bulbs. After examining the bulbs' colors, sizes, shapes, and textures, challenge them to sort the bulbs into groups. Explain to your young learners that these particular bulbs can be eaten just as sprouts can be eaten, but that some bulbs are poisonous. Encourage your little ones to ask their parents for tastes of edible bulbs at home!

## An Inside Study of Onions

Have your little scientists investigate the insides of onions and then make onion prints! Before the activity, cut a yellow, white, and red onion in half horizontally. Enclose each onion half in a resealable plastic bag. To begin the activity, have each child study and compare the inside moist layers with the outer papery layers of each onion half. Next, remove each onion from its bag and insert a fork for a handle as shown. Invite each child to don a pair of safety glasses and then dip each type of onion into a shallow pan of tempera paint and then make prints on a sheet of construction paper. Lead students to the conclusion that onions can be different sizes and shapes. As a finishing touch, display these colorful prints around your room. Ooh-la-la—onions!

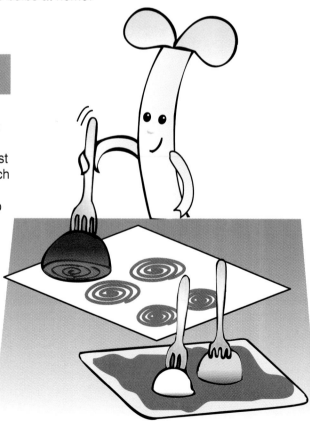

### Did You Know?
A bulb is a thick, fleshy plant bud under the soil that stores food for the plant. Not all bulbs are edible; most flowering bulbs are poisonous.

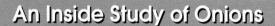

## Sprouting Bulbs

Your little ones will be amazed to discover that edible bulbs sprout, too! In advance, have parents donate a class supply of garlic bulbs. Personalize an eight-ounce clear plastic cup for each child. Cut a class supply of foam circles to fit inside the cups as shown. Next, cut an *X* in the center of each circle, just large enough for a garlic clove to be inserted without falling out. Have a small group of students examine the garlic heads, compare them with onions, and then break the garlic heads apart to reveal individual cloves. Initiate a discussion about whether the cloves are alive or not. Then use the directions below to have your students complete the experiment. Roots and sprouts will appear in approximately three days. Use the newly sprouted cloves in "Sprout Portraits" below.

### Directions:

1. Peel the papery layer from a garlic clove.
2. Gently push your clove, pointed end up, into the *X* in a foam circle.
3. Fill your cup halfway with water. Put the circle in your cup. Make sure that the bottom of the clove is in the water.
4. Set your cup near a sunny window, and check each day for any changes.
5. Add water as needed to keep the bottom of the clove wet.

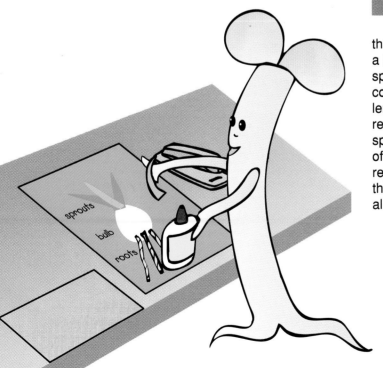

## Sprout Portraits

Use the sprouts from "Sprouting Bulbs" as models for this scientific diagram activity. To make one diagram, use a bulb-shaped sponge and white tempera paint to make a sponge print in the center of a 6" x 9" sheet of colored construction paper. When the paint is dry, glue several 2" lengths of white yarn to the bottom of the bulb print to resemble roots. Next, glue several green tissue paper sprouts to the top of the bulb print. Staple a 4" x 6" piece of waxed paper across the bottom portion of the paper to represent water; then have students label the parts of their bulbs as shown. Display these sprouting portraits for all to see!

### Did You Know?

A head of garlic is a bulb. Each small clove is a separate bulb. Garlic and onions are examples of edible bulbs.

## Bulbs A-bloomin'!

Your little ones will bloom with enthusiasm as they learn about inedible bulbs that sprout flowers! In advance, purchase an inexpensive pot of blooming daffodils, tulips, or hyacinths. Have your students describe the plant parts. Then have them brainstorm what might be underneath the soil. Remove two of the flowers with their bulbs intact. Split one bulb in half lengthwise; then invite students to examine both bulbs.

If you already have small spring flowering bulbs such as paperwhites or hyacinths, extend your inedible bulb study by forcing the bulbs to bloom. Place the bulbs in a paper bag and store them in the refrigerator for four to six weeks. To sprout a chilled bulb, set it in the mouth of a narrow, water-filled, clear plastic jar so that only the rounded base of the bulb is submerged. Encourage your youngsters to discuss the daily changes that they observe. Grow, flowers, grow!

## Sprouting Is Tops!

Not only seeds and bulbs sprout! Demonstrate to your little ones that some vegetable tops will sprout and grow if sunlight and water are provided. To prepare for this activity, remove the greens from two red beets and two carrots; then cut them two inches down from their crowns. Fill two shallow pans with gravel and water. Put a carrot and a beet, cut side down, into each pan. Place one pan near a warm, sunny window and the other in a cool, dark place. Make sure to water the vegetable tops daily. When the window vegetables have sprouted leaves (approximately three to six days), compare the two pans. Lead your little scientists to conclude that vegetable tops need a supply of bright, warm light to grow!

## Sprouts All About

Culminate this unit by having your little learners make these smashing sprout booklets. In advance, duplicate pages 17 and 18 onto white construction paper to make a class supply; then cut the pages apart. Gather the necessary supplies and then use the suggestions below to help each student complete a booklet. Have each child sequence her pages and staple them behind the cover on the left-hand side. Read all about sprouts!

**Cover:** Print your name on the line. Draw and then color several seeds and bulbs.
**Page 1:** Glue on a 2" square of paper towel. Use a cotton swab to paint seeds on the towel. Use a green marker to draw a sprout growing from each seed.
**Page 2:** Cut out the cup pattern and glue it to the page. Use a blue crayon to color water in the cup. Glue on pieces of string for roots. Draw a sprout.
**Page 3:** Make an orange carrot-top print in the dish. Draw green leaves sprouting from the carrot top.
**Page 4:** Color the flower pattern red or blue and then cut it out. Glue the flower stem where indicated so that it extends above the top of the page. Then fold the flower down. Use a gray or black washable ink pad to make fingerprints in the pan to resemble gravel.

# What Will Sprout?

by _____

©2000 The Education Center, Inc. • *Science for All Seasons* • *Spring* • TEC3049

## Seeds
and beans
will sprout.

**1.**

## Garlic
will sprout too.

Glue cup here.

**2.**

## Booklet Pages and Patterns
Use with "Sprouts All About" on page 16.

Carrot
tops
will sprout.

**3.**

A flower
bulb will sprout.
Will it be
red or blue?

Glue
here.

**4.**

cup

flower

©2000 The Education Center, Inc. • *Science for All Seasons* • *Spring* • TEC3049

# Give Me Five for Snacktime!

Focus your scientific studies on the five senses with these mouthwatering activities!

## Calling All Senses!

Your little ones will be in touch with their senses as they investigate this surprise snack! In advance, duplicate the recording sheet on page 22 for each student. Put a class supply of jelly beans plus several extras into a paper lunch bag. To begin the activity, sing the song below with a small group of students. Shake the bag, having students silently guess what is inside by listening. Next, give each child a recording sheet; then have her draw a picture of her guess in the first box. Sing the song again, substituting *smelling* for the underlined words. Following the same sensory process, have each child sniff her bag and then draw a picture of her guess. Continue in this manner until all five sensory guesses have been recorded. Discovery has never "bean" so much fun!

*(sung to the tune of "Are You Sleeping?")*

Can you guess? Can you guess?
What's inside? What's inside?
Do you know by [listening]?
Do you know by [listening]?
What's inside? What's inside?

## All Eyes on Color!

This center idea will have your little scientists seeing colors in a new way! In advance, stock a center with empty egg cartons and several small bowls of Froot Loops® cereal. (Be sure to have extras nearby for munching.) When a child visits this center, have him sort a bowl of cereal by placing each different color into a separate carton compartment. Next, have him use his sense of sight to identify the dark and light colors. Then have him count the cereal pieces in each carton compartment. After he compares each one, have the student put the cereal pieces back in the bowl. Give a high five for eyes!

### This Is Why

The cereal pieces could be sorted by color because *cones* in the eye tell the brain what color they are. *Rods* detect only black and white.

## Who "Nose" This Familiar Smell?

Youngsters will delight in sniffing out a mystery smell! To prepare, make popcorn while your students are out of the room. As soon as your students enter the room, ask them to guess the mystery aroma; then have them discuss and compare the smell with pizza, tacos, and chocolate cake. Next, have students discuss different smells found in various places, such as at home, at the zoo, and at a restaurant. Explain to your little learners that their noses and brains work together to identify each smell, even if they can't see, touch, taste, or hear the object. Invite students to taste the freshly popped popcorn. You're sure to see many noses wiggling to get a good whiff of the scrumptious aroma!

When it's dinnertime, what smells yummy?
What smells so good you want to put it in your tummy?

Name: Donny

Chicken and rice _____ smells yummy!

## Home Learning Lab

Strengthen the home-school connection with this aromatic activity. In advance, duplicate page 23 to send home with each student. Encourage each child to go on a food-sniffing adventure with a parent and then draw a food that represents his favorite food aroma on his paper (or glue on a magazine picture). When all the papers have been returned, gather your students and invite them to share their completed pages. Then stack all the pages between two covers and bind them along the left-hand side. Place this book in your class library and encourage your youngsters to sniff out some good reading!

## Sweet or Sour?

Involve your students in some sweet, sour, salty, and bitter taste testing! In advance, put each of the following in a separate bowl: sugar, salt, unsweetened lemonade drink powder, and unsweetened cocoa. Program an 8½" x 11" sheet of paper to resemble the tasting mat shown; then duplicate it to make a class supply. Give each student a mat, and put a small amount of one ingredient in the first section. Ask each child to examine the ingredient and predict the flavor. Then invite him to sprinkle a small pinch of the ingredient on his tongue and identify its taste as sweet, sour, salty, or bitter. Continue the activity until all four ingredients have been tried. Discuss students' predictions with their results. Your budding scientists will be amazed at what taste buds can do!

# Tasty Textures

This discovery activity will introduce your little ones to a variety of tempting textures! In advance, have parents donate a jar of creamy peanut butter, a large container of vanilla yogurt, a box of saltine crackers, a box of chewy granola bars, small paper plates, and plastic spoons. Duplicate and then cut apart the response sheets on page 24 to make a class supply. To begin the activity, have students brainstorm crunchy, soft, and chewy foods; record their responses on a piece of chart paper. At snacktime, have each child sample the foods; then have her compare their textures. Give each child a response sheet; then help her record her response. Next, instruct the child to draw a food with her favorite texture in the bubble. Then have her draw a picture of herself (or glue a small photo) in the rectangle. Display the completed projects on a bulletin board. Then use the display as a discussion guide to determine the class's favorite textures. No doubt about it—textures are terrific!

Each kind of food is such a treat. But a ___chewy___ (texture) ___granola bar___ (food) is what I like to eat!

## This Is Why

Crunching can be heard because of sound waves. The waves enter the ear and hit the eardrum, making it vibrate.

# Noisy Nibblers

Combine the senses of hearing and taste and what do you get? Lots of delicious crunching and munching! Gather your students and review the list of crunchy foods generated in "Tasty Textures." Then give each child an apple slice. On the count of three, have each child take a bite out of his slice. Invite students to discuss what kinds of sounds they heard (crunching, popping, snapping, etc.). Next, sing the song below with your students, each time substituting a different crunchy food in place of the underlined word. Crunch, crunch!

*(sung to the tune of "Pop Goes the Weasel")*

Did you know that some foods crunch?
You'll hear them loud and clear.
Bite an [apple]—crunch, crunch, crunch!
Music to my ears!

# "Sense-ational" Snacks

Culminate this unit with a flavorful snack that combines all five senses. To make one snack portion, have each child put five of each ingredient listed below into a resealable plastic bag. Have her seal the bag and then shake it gently to listen to the sound. Have her use her sense of sight to select an ingredient. Next, have her feel its texture. After she smells the treat, invite her to taste it. Gimme five!

mini marshmallows
raisins
Skittles® candies
cereal pieces
salted peanuts
semisweet mini chocolate chips

# Give Me Five!

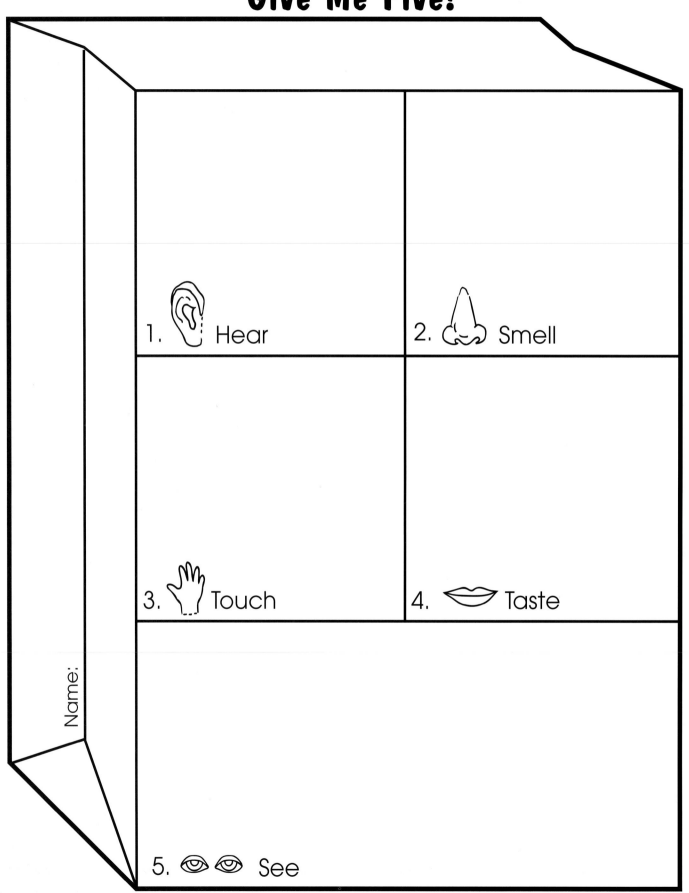

1. Hear

2. Smell

3. Touch

4. Taste

Name:

5. See

# A Full Plate

Dear Parent,

   We are learning about the five senses in school! Read the poem below with your child and then go on a food-sniffing adventure to find delicious smells in your kitchen. Next, have your child draw a picture on the plate or cut out and glue a magazine picture of a food that smells yummy. Help your child print his or her name on the plate and the name of the food on the line. Return this sheet to school by _____.

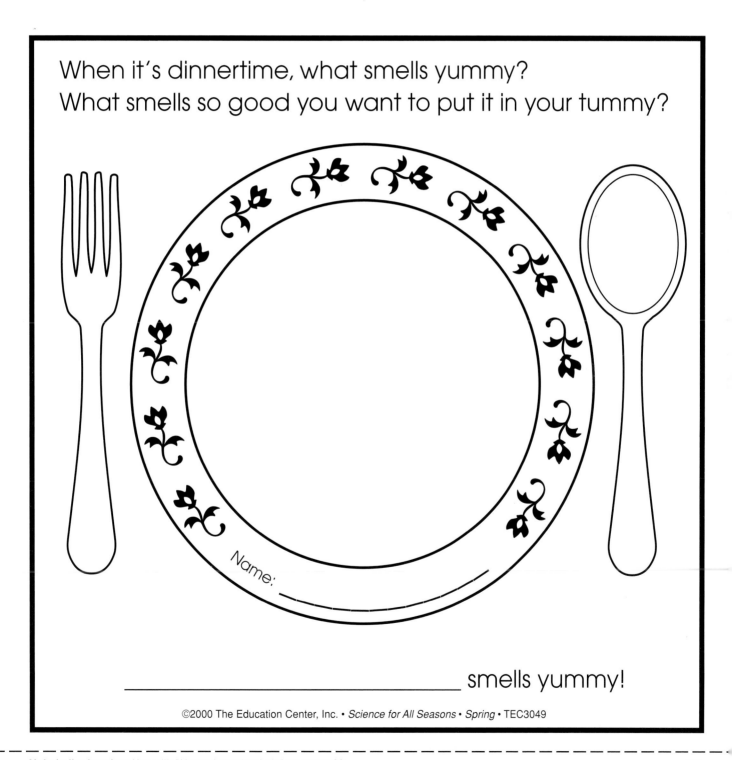

When it's dinnertime, what smells yummy?
What smells so good you want to put it in your tummy?

Name: _____

_____ smells yummy!

# Response Sheets

Use with "Tasty Textures" on page 21.

Each kind of food is such a treat.
But a _____ _____ is what I like to eat!
   (texture)              (food)

Each kind of food is such a treat.
But a _____ _____ is what I like to eat!
   (texture)              (food)

# Soil Search

Invite your little ones to dig in and explore a very down-to-earth topic—soil!

## An Earthy Mystery

Challenge your youngsters to unearth a scientific mystery with this inference activity. To prepare, cover a small oatmeal container and its lid with construction paper. Place two cups of garden soil in the container; then tightly secure the lid with tape. Begin the activity by seating your little scientists in a circle. Tell students that they are going to be learning about the mystery substance inside the container. Pass the container around the circle so that each child can feel its weight and listen as she shakes the container. Next, give students a few more clues about the container's contents by chanting the following riddle:

> What is inside? What did I hide?
> Its color is brown. To see it, look down.
> It's crumbly and dry. It's not in the sky!
> It's all around...on the ground!

After each youngster has had a chance to guess the contents of the container, remove the lid and pass it around so that everyone can take a peek. Aha!

## What do we know about soil?

It's brown. –Leah

If you put water in it, you can make mud. –Aaron

Plants grow in it. –Dustin

My dog likes to dig in it! –Kasey

## Soil Exploration

Encourage your little ones to get down to the nitty-gritty of soil exploration with this hands-on investigation. To prepare, purchase a bag of garden soil at a garden center or discount store. Dump the soil into your sensory table and add some toy shovels and plastic cups. Then gather your group and ask them to tell you what they know about soil. Record their responses on a sheet of chart paper labeled as shown. Next, invite small groups to visit the sensory table to explore the appearance and texture of the soil. Encourage students' observations by asking questions. How does the soil smell? What does the soil feel like? What kind of things do you see in the soil? After everyone has had a chance to visit this down-and-dirty center, regroup and ask students to tell you more about soil; add the new observations to your chart. Then display the chart in your classroom. And keep a pen handy—your young scientists will have new discoveries to add!

## A Soil Profile

Dig deeper in your soil search as you and your students make a model of the soil's layers. First, divide your class into three groups and give each group a large zippered plastic bag. Head outdoors and ask one group to hunt for rocks, another group to dig up some dirt, and the third group to gather decaying plant material, such as dead leaves or twigs. Return to your classroom and compare the weight, texture, and color of the materials in the three bags.

Next, bring out a large, clean, empty peanut butter jar. Explain that, together, you're going to build a model of what some soil looks like below the ground. Have student volunteers first put the rocks in the jar, then add a middle layer of dirt, and then put the plant matter on top. Explain that soil has a rocky underlayer, topped by a layer of dirt *(topsoil)*, and finished on the surface with a thin layer of decaying plant material *(humus)* that helps make the soil rich and healthy for plant growth. Place the lid on the jar and keep it on display for little ones to study. Then teach your students the "Soil Layers Song" on this page to reinforce the demonstration.

### Did You Know?

Humus is created when plant and animal materials decay. Humus enriches the topsoil with nutrients important to plants. It also improves the ability of the topsoil to absorb water.

## Soil Layers Song

*(sung to the tune of "Down at the Station")*

Here is the soil that's all made up of layers.
There are special layers stacked up here to see.
See the <u>rocks and stones</u> here in the bottom
   layer?
Soil has layers—one, two, three!

Here is the soil that's all made up of layers.
There are special layers stacked up here to see.
See the <u>topsoil</u> that's in the middle layer?
Soil has layers—one, two, three!

Here is the soil that's all made up of layers.
There are special layers stacked up here to see.
See the <u>humus</u> here that's in the tip-top layer?
Soil has layers—one, two, three!

## Soil Profile Poster

Now that your little ones have helped make a model of the soil, they're ready to make these soil profile posters of their own. For each child, photocopy pages 29, 30, and 31 on white paper. Ask each child to cut out the layer labels on page 31; then guide him to glue each label to the corresponding box on his reproducibles. Next, have each child follow the instructions below to complete each poster panel. Once the child has decorated his panels, have him cut out each one along the heavy outline. Then help him glue his panels together as indicated.

**Title Panel:** Color the panel blue. Write your name on the line.
**Panel 1:** Draw a flower center just above the stem tip. Glue paper flower petals around the center. Color the background blue.
**Panel 2:** Color the stem and leaves green and the background blue. Glue bits of torn green, yellow, and brown paper to the panel on each side of the stem.
**Panel 3:** Color the roots tan. Color the background brown.
**Panel 4:** Color the background brown. Make black thumbprint "rocks" on the panel.

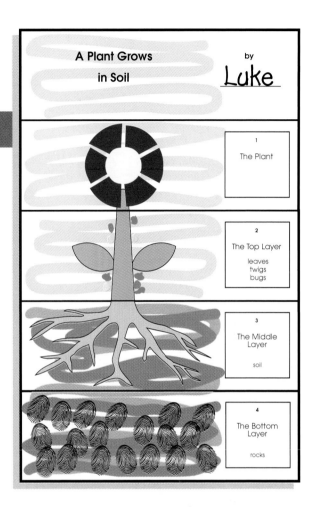

A Plant Grows in Soil   by Luke

1 The Plant

2 The Top Layer
leaves
twigs
bugs

3 The Middle Layer
soil

4 The Bottom Layer
rocks

## Luscious Layers

Mmm…*these* soil layers make quite a snack! Help each child in a small group prepare her snack; then prompt her to compare it to the layers on her soil profile poster before taking a bite.

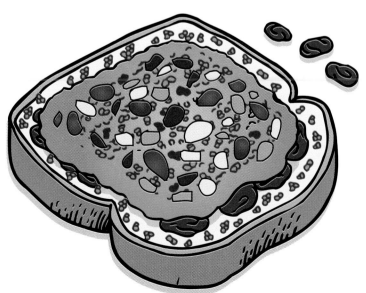

### Soil Layers Sandwich

**Ingredients (for one):**
1 slice of wheat bread
2 tablespoons raisins
chunky peanut butter
2 cinnamon bite-sized graham snacks
2 chocolate bite-sized graham snacks

**Supplies:**
paper plate
plastic knife
plastic sandwich bag

**To make one soil layers sandwich:**
1. Put the bread on a paper plate.
2. Sprinkle the raisins on the bread.
3. Spread peanut butter over the raisins.
4. Put the four graham snacks in a plastic sandwich bag and crush them.
5. Sprinkle the crushed grahams over the peanut butter.

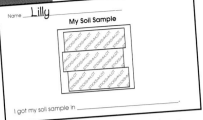

Name __Lilly__

**My Soil Sample**

I got my soil sample in _____

before

Name __Lilly__

**My Soil Sample**

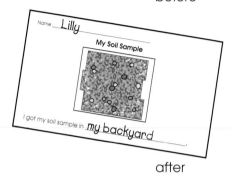

I got my soil sample in __my backyard__

after

## Home Learning Lab

Encourage youngsters to collect and compare different types of soil with this home activity. Duplicate page 32 for each child. Stick three 2½-inch strips of ¾-inch-wide double-stick poster tape inside the square on each child's sheet. Leave the peel-off covering intact on the exposed side of the tape. Place each child's sheet in a large zippered plastic bag and send it home. When students return their sheets to school, allow them to share their findings. Help each child cut off the bottom half of her sheet; then have the students work together to sort similar samples into piles. What kind of soil is most common in *your* neighborhood?

## Soil Sorting

Ground your youngsters in the basics of classification with this soil-sorting activity. To prepare, gather several different kinds of soil, such as packaged garden soil, peat moss, potting soil, and plain sand. Divide *each* type of soil you've collected into three zippered freezer bags. Use clear packing tape to securely seal the top of each bag and prevent leaks. Then load all the bags into a child's wheelbarrow or wagon and wheel them into a center, along with a plastic flowerpot for each type of soil.

To use this center, a pair of youngsters studies the bags and groups together those that are alike, placing each group into a separate flowerpot. Once all your little ones have had a chance to try their hand at soil sorting, mix all the soils together and put some of the mix into each flowerpot. Add some flower seeds, a sprinkle of water, and the loving attention of your soil experts. You'll soon see your room in bloom!

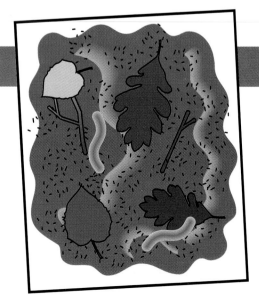

## A Spectacular Soil Display

Wrap up your soil study with a delightful display of earthy items! First, have youngsters create fingerpaintings with brown paint. While the paint is still wet, sprinkle the contents of a dry tea bag over each child's painting. When the paint is dry, invite her to glue on a few twigs and leaves, and perhaps even a few pipe cleaner "worms"! Display the completed collages on a bulletin board. Position a table in front of the board and cover it with brown bulletin board paper. Display some books about soil, your flowerpots filled with soil (and maybe some sprouts!) from "Soil Sorting," and your soil profile jar (see "A Soil Profile" on page 26). Then hang your students' soil profile posters (page 27) all around the board to complete this educational exhibit about the science of soil!

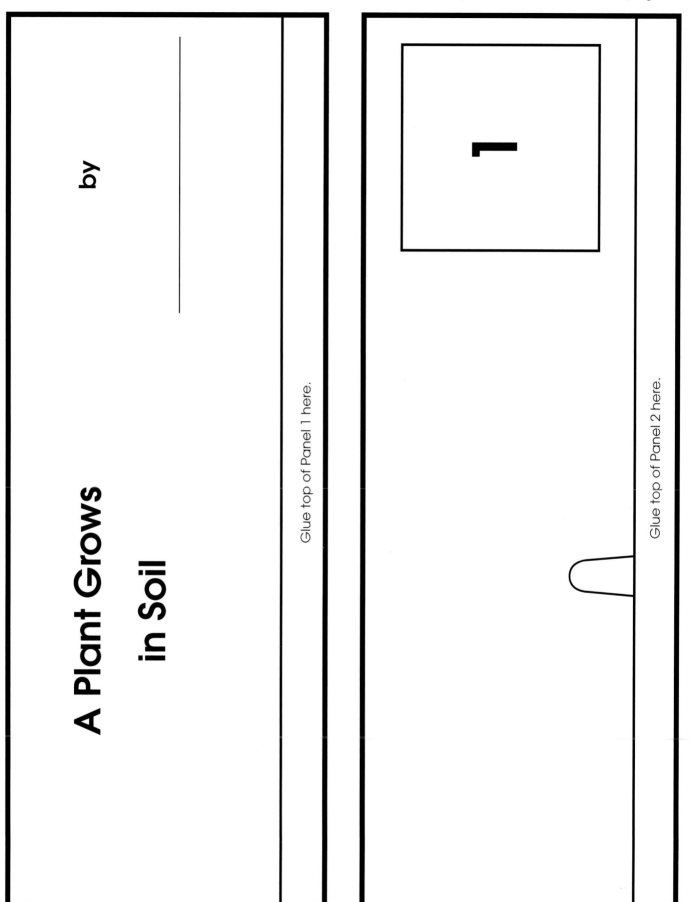

A Plant Grows
in Soil

by

Glue top of Panel 1 here.

Glue top of Panel 2 here.

# Poster Panels

Use with "Soil Profile Poster" on page 27.

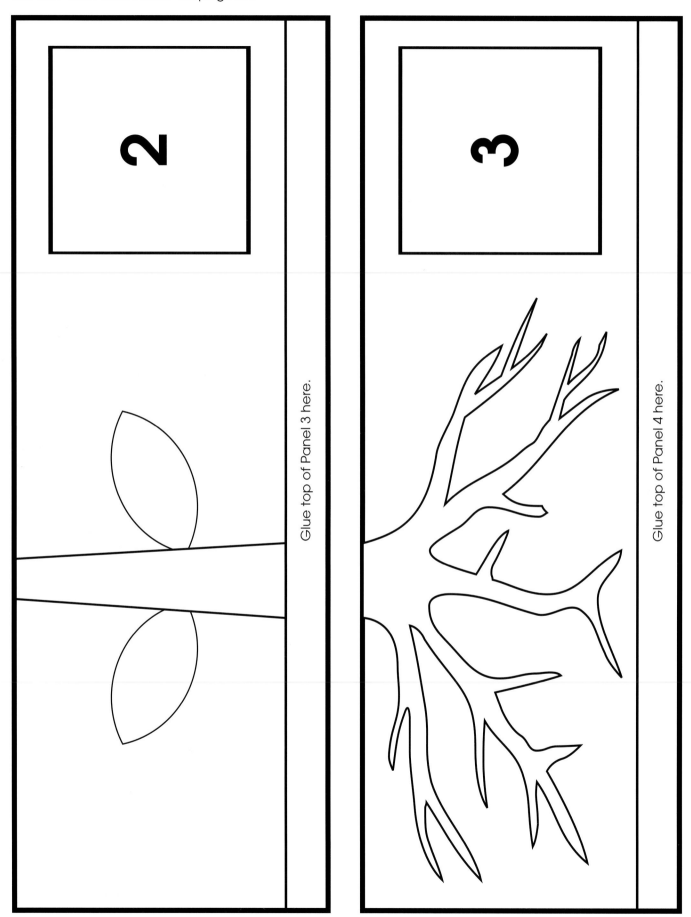

4

1

**The Plant**

2

**The Top Layer**

leaves
twigs
bugs

3

**The Middle
Layer**

soil

4

**The Bottom
Layer**

rocks

# Dear Parent,

We have been learning about soil at school. Please help your child follow the directions below to collect a soil sample from your yard, from a park, or from a neighborhood garden.

1. Find the soil you wish to sample.
2. Remove the peel-off covering from the tape inside the square.
3. Lay this paper facedown on the soil so that the sticky tape is touching the soil. Press down on the paper.
4. Put the paper back in the zippered plastic bag. Return it to school by

_____.
(date)

Thank you!

- - - - - - - - - - - - - - - - - - - - - - - - - - - - - - - - - - - - - - - - - -

Name _____

## My Soil Sample

I got my soil sample in _____.

- - - - - - - - - - - - - - - - - - - - - - - - - - - - - - - - - - - - - - - - - -

**Note to the teacher:** Use with "Home Learning Lab" on page 28.

# A-Tisket, A-Tasket—Learn About Baskets

A basketful of surprises awaits your little ones as they explore these commonly seen springtime objects.

## Getting Ready

In preparation for this unit, you'll need to borrow a bushel of beautiful baskets! Duplicate the parent note on page 36 to make a class supply. Send a note home with each child a few days (or weeks) before beginning this unit. Tag each borrowed basket, using a ribbon personalized with the lender's name. You'll also want to stock your classroom with unusual baskets, such as laundry baskets, open mesh baskets, old-fashioned strawberry baskets (if you have a supply) and toy shopping baskets.

## Yes or No?

What makes a basket a basket? Set the stage for learning by inviting your young scientists to investigate some characteristics of these woven containers. Begin by gathering a paper bag, a plastic bowl, a handleless basket, a woven basket with handles, and a box. Display each object one at a time and ask your crew if it is a basket. Encourage youngsters to answer "yes" or "no" for each item; then lead a discussion about what makes a container a basket. Jot student responses on a basket-shaped chart. Wrap up this activity by explaining that a basket is a container that is usually made of interwoven materials such as wood, plastic, or reeds.

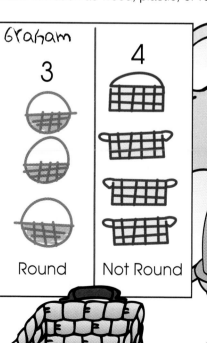

Graham

3 — Round

4 — Not Round

## Basket Graphs

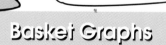

After you've borrowed a supply of baskets (see "Getting Ready"), weave a few graphing experiences into your day. During a circle time, invite youngsters to sort the baskets into groups according to one attribute (such as round or not round, handles or no handles, etc.). Discuss the results, and then give each child a blank, two-column bar graph and help her record the findings. Later, place the baskets, a supply of blank graphs, and crayons in a center so youngsters can further explore them. Wow—there sure are a lot of round baskets!

## Alike and Different

Here's an activity that reinforces visual discrimination and attribute identification, and even stimulates creative language. Gather three different types of baskets, such as one with handles, one that's very loosely woven, and one made of plastic. Show them to your group as you sing this song to the tune of "Ten Little Indians."

One little, two little, three little baskets.
What do we know about these baskets?
What's [the same] about these baskets?
Let's check them out and see!

Discuss how the baskets are the same. (If necessary, prompt students to decide whether each basket is carried the same way and so forth.) Sing the song again, substituting *same* with *different*. Encourage students to describe ways in which the baskets are different, including attributes such as shape, color, and material.

## Home Learning Lab

Now that your little ones are familiar with different types of baskets, weave families into the fun with this basket scavenger hunt! Duplicate the recording sheet (page 37) to make a class supply; then send a copy home with each child. As the sheets are returned, encourage each child to share her findings with the class. Invite students to compare the basket rubbings for similarities and differences.

## Hold It!

Here's the perfect small-group activity to capture the imaginations of your lively little learners! In advance, gather one open-weave basket (metal mesh baskets or old-fashioned strawberry baskets are ideal) for each child in a small group. Place a variety of materials—such as rice, paper clips, glitter, jelly beans, counting manipulatives, crayons, clothespins, and buttons—within easy reach of your group. Challenge each youngster to predict which objects her basket will hold and which objects will fall through; then invite her to test her predictions. Conclude the activity by asking youngsters to brainstorm why some baskets are made with open grids.

## Did You Know?

A container, such as a basket, is designed for the object it is intended to hold. Some baskets are designed with open grids on the sides and bottom to allow air to circulate around the contents, keeping them fresh.

What Does
**My Basket**
Hold?
by
*Katie*

It holds an egg.  1

but it doesn't hold rice.  2

It holds strawberries,  3

but it doesn't hold glue.  4

It holds a chocolate bunny,  5

but it doesn't hold glitter.  6

It holds a *cookie*  7

# What Does My Basket Hold?

After experimenting with open-weave baskets in "Hold It!" (page 34), your group will enjoy putting together this nifty booklet about their discoveries. In advance, duplicate the patterns and booklet pages on pages 38–42 to make a class set. Also cut a three-inch square of construction paper for each child. Begin by having each child color and cut out the patterns on page 42. Help each child cut apart her booklet pages. Then encourage her to complete them according to the suggestions below. Have each child sequence her pages and staple them behind the cover. Invite each child to read her booklet with classmates and then take it home to share with family members. Now that's a bushel of bookmaking fun!

**Cover:** Write your name on the line.
**Page 1:** Staple a basket pattern to the page. Slip the egg pattern into the basket.
**Page 2:** Glue rice below the basket.
**Page 3:** Staple a basket pattern to the page. Tuck the strawberry pattern into the basket.
**Page 4:** Spread tinted glue below the basket.
**Page 5:** Staple a basket pattern to the page. Slip the bunny pattern into the basket.
**Page 6:** Glue glitter below the basket.
**Page 7:** Staple a basket pattern to the page. Using the construction paper square, color, cut, and glue a picture of an object that will fit in your basket. Write its name on the line.

# Snack in a Basket

Now that your tykes have plenty of experience with baskets, it's time for them to make some of their own. In advance, collect a 64-ounce milk or juice carton for each child. Cut off the top half of each carton; then spray-paint the carton bottoms with bright spring colors. When the paint is dry, use a craft knife to make an odd number of equally spaced, vertical slits in each side of each carton. (Adjust the number of slits based on each child's fine-motor skills.) Also cut four to five one-foot lengths of wide fabric ribbon for each child.

To make a basket, each child tapes one end of a ribbon length between two of the carton's slits. He weaves the ribbon in and out of the slits, turning the basket as he goes. When he comes to the end of a ribbon length, he tapes it to the basket and begins weaving again with a new ribbon. He staples the last ribbon length over the top of the basket to create a handle. Then he fills the basket with crinkle paper or plastic grass. Later, when your group is out of the classroom, put an individually wrapped snack in each basket for a fun springtime treat!

# A-tisket, a-tasket,
# Please bring some kind of basket!

Dear Parent,
   We are going to be sorting and classifying baskets at school. Do you have a basket we can borrow for our studies? If so, please send it by

_____ .

(date)

Thanks!

# A-tisket, a-tasket,
# Please bring some kind of basket!

Dear Parent,
   We are going to be sorting and classifying baskets at school. Do you have a basket we can borrow for our studies? If so, please send it by

_____ .

(date)

Thanks!

# Basket Scavenger Hunt

Dear Parent,

    We have been sorting and classifying baskets at school. How many baskets are in your home? Go on an indoor scavenger hunt with your child to find out! Then help your child report your findings below. (Use a dark crayon to make the rubbing.)

We counted _____.

Here is a rubbing of a basket.

# What Does
# My Basket
## Hold?

## by

_____

Staple basket here.

## It holds an egg,

1

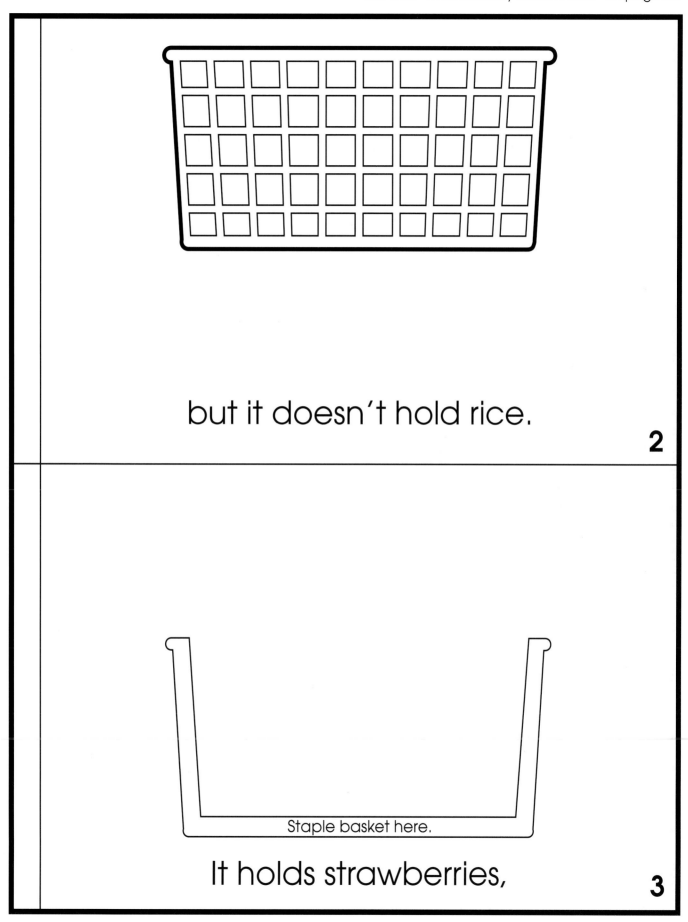

but it doesn't hold rice.

**2**

Staple basket here.

It holds strawberries,

**3**

but it doesn't hold glue.

4

Staple basket here.

It holds a chocolate bunny,

5

but it doesn't hold glitter.

6

Staple basket here.

It holds a _____.

7

# Patterns
Use with "What Does My Basket Hold?" on page 35.

## basket patterns

egg

chocolate bunny

strawberries

# Science Book Spectrum

# Spring Selections

Help your little ones greet the coming of spring with these seasonal stories.

## When Spring Comes

Written and Photo-Illustrated by Robert Maass
Published by Henry Holt and Company

Springtime is the right time for your budding scientists to observe the world around them. *When Spring Comes* blooms with colorful photos and descriptions of springtime sights. Read the book aloud, allowing time for students to comment on the spring objects and activities in the story. After you've read and discussed the book, encourage your youngsters to dictate a list of other sights they might see in the spring. Then help students classify the sights under separate headings such as "Plants and Flowers," "Outdoor Activities," "Weather," and "Baby Animals." Later, invite each child to fill a minibooklet with her favorite signs of spring. Duplicate the booklet pattern (page 45) on white paper for each child. Have the child cut out her booklet cover and pages, sequence them, and then staple the resulting booklet in the upper-left corner. Encourage each child to personalize her booklet by illustrating each page with a "favorite thing" to complement the text. Conclude the activity by inviting each child to read her booklet aloud so that she can share her favorite springtime observations with classmates.

| Spring Sights | | | |
| --- | --- | --- | --- |
| Plants and Flowers | Outdoor Activities | Weather | Baby Animals |
| strawberries tulips dogwoods grass | T-ball soccer hiking flying a kite | rain wind sun | rabbits lambs puppies robins |

## In the Rain With Baby Duck

Written by Amy Hest
Illustrated by Jill Barton
Published by Candlewick Press

Baby Duck's reaction to a rainstorm almost ruins her day, but Grampa Duck remembers that sometimes it takes special rain gear to make wet weather feel wonderful! After sharing this tale with your youngsters, invite them to discuss what rain gear helps them stay nice and dry in a spring shower. Encourage each child to predict which color of raincoat is the most popular in the class. Then follow up with this graphing activity. Give each child a copy of the survey recording sheet (page 46) and help him complete the top portion. Next, ask him to color the large raincoat at the bottom of the page to look like his own; then have him cut it out and post it on a prepared graph. Invite students to discuss the completed graph and decide which color of raincoat is the most popular. Then have each child return to his survey sheet and record the most popular raincoat color. Your little ones will eagerly look forward to showing off their colorful gear on the next rainy day!

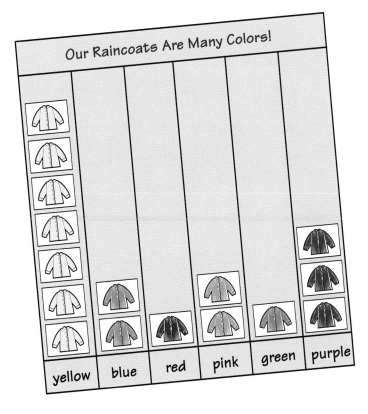

Our Raincoats Are Many Colors!

yellow  blue  red  pink  green  purple

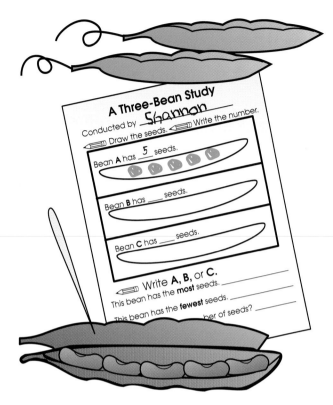

A Three-Bean Study
Conducted by __Shannon__
Draw the seeds. Write the number.

Bean A has __5__ seeds.

Bean B has ____ seeds.

Bean C has ____ seeds.

Write A, B, or C.
This bean has the **most** seeds. ____
This bean has the **fewest** seeds. ____

## One Bean

Written by Anne Rockwell
Illustrated by Megan Halsey
Published by Walker and Company

Sprout some fun when you share *One Bean,* a step-by-step story that centers around a simple little legume. As you read the book, discuss the similarities of the bean sprout with the sprouts studied in the "Little Sprouts Science" unit (pages 13–18). After reading, return to the page that describes what the boy sees when he investigates the inside of a ripe green bean. Next, show students a bowl of fresh, raw green beans, and ask them if they think they will find the same kinds of little seeds inside. Then invite each child to take her own peek inside beans with this engaging activity!

Give each child three green beans, a copy of the lab report on page 47, and a toothpick. Demonstrate how to use the toothpick to split open a beanpod and count the seeds. Instruct each child to draw a matching number of seeds inside bean A on her lab report. Then have her repeat the process for each remaining bean. Help her use the data to draw conclusions and then complete her report. Wrap up the activity by compiling the seed data to discover the greatest, fewest, and most common number of seeds in your students' supply of green beans.

## A Nest Full of Eggs

Written by Priscilla Belz Jenkins
Illustrated by Lizzy Rockwell
Published by HarperCollins Children's Books

There's nothing like watching the robins build their safe, cozy nests from common materials each spring. After you've read aloud *A Nest Full of Eggs,* review the nest-building pictures. Have students list items that the robins used to build their nest. Then stock a nest-making center with those materials as well as shredded newspaper, yarn, string, crinkled paper strips, and Easter grass. Provide each child in this center with a personalized, individual-sized pie tin, a paintbrush, and a squeeze bottle of brown-tinted glue.

To make one robin's nest craft, squeeze an amount of glue into the pie tin and spread it around with the paintbrush to coat the interior. Press into the glue a slightly overlapping layer of nest materials; then set it aside to dry. Glue a second layer of materials to the nest, building it into a cup shape as described in the book. When the nest is dry, gently press the sides of the child's pan to loosen the nest and remove it. To complete the activity, duplicate the nest materials recording sheet (page 48) on brown paper to make a class supply. Ask each little builder to glue a sample of her preferred nest materials to the sheet. Arrange each child's nest model along with her recording sheet on a table to create a constructive display!

Here Is the Nest That __Kayla__ Built!

My nest is made of **mud** and...

2

Here's an outside game I like to play.

5

My favorite sign of

spring is _____.

1

It's a baby animal's birthday.

4

brings a Maytime flower.

Signs
of
Spring

by _____

3

A soft April shower...

Name _____

# My Rain Gear Survey

 **Circle** the items that you use.

hat                boots                umbrella                raincoat

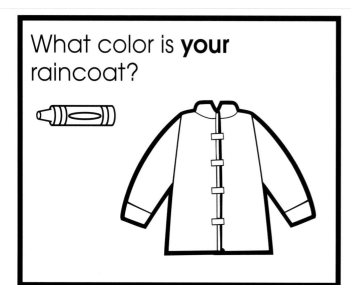

What color is **your** raincoat?

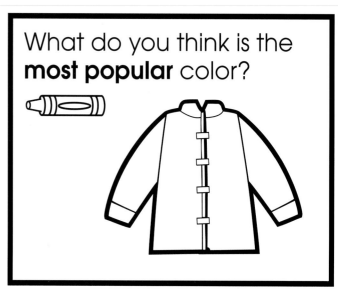

What do you think is the **most popular** color?

The most popular raincoat color in our class is...

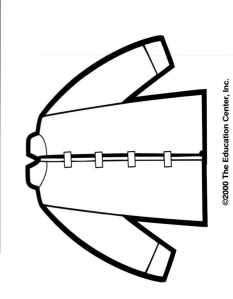 Write.

_____

- - - - - - - - - - - - - - - - - - - - -

_____

Name

# A Three-Bean Study

Conducted by _____

✏️ Draw the seeds.　　✏️ Write the number.

Bean **A** has _____ seeds.

Bean **B** has _____ seeds.

Bean **C** has _____ seeds.

✏️ Write **A, B,** or **C.**

This bean has the **most** seeds. _____

This bean has the **fewest** seeds. _____

Do any beans have the **same** number of seeds? _____

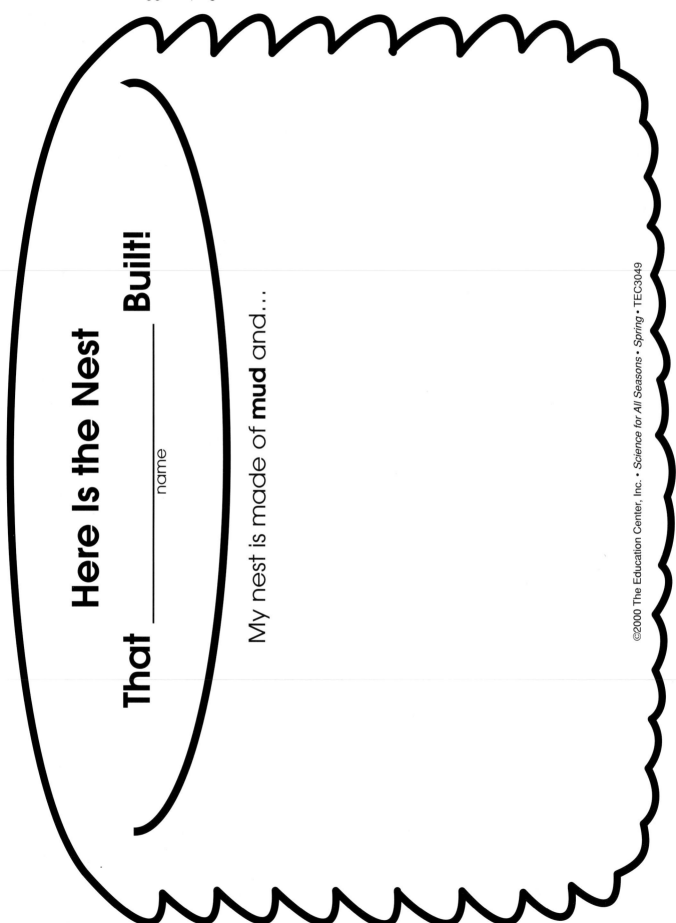

**Here Is the Nest**

**That _____ Built!**

name

My nest is made of **mud** and...

# The Scientific Artist

## The Scientific Artist Investigates Crayons

Red, yellow, green, purple, orange, and blue. This colorful unit is ready for you!

Color your young scientists curious when you begin your crayon studies with this inference activity. In advance, place a crayon in a paper lunch bag. Rattle the bag to attract youngsters' attention; then sing the song below. Then dramatically read each of the clues to your youngsters; after revealing each one, encourage them to guess the bag's contents.

*(sung to the tune of "The Wheels on the Bus")*

What's in the bag? Oh, can you guess?
Can you guess? Can you guess?
What's in the bag? Oh, can you guess?
Here are some clues.

**Clues:**
1. It's small enough to be in this bag.
2. When I use it, it gets smaller and smaller.
3. It is usually wrapped in paper.
4. Sometimes it breaks.
5. It comes in different colors.
6. You can draw, write, and color with it.

Invite youngsters to take one last guess, then reveal the bag's contents: It's a crayon, of course! Reread the clues to confirm that they do indeed describe a crayon.

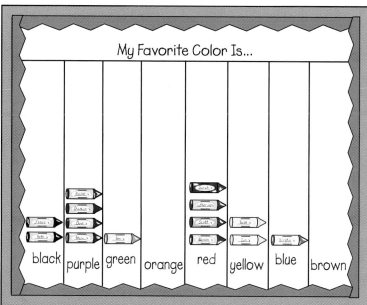

## And the Winner Is...

Crayons come in many beautiful hues, but everyone has a special favorite! Predicting and comparing are just a couple of the skills involved in this colorful graphing idea. In advance, prepare a large graph by labeling it with the eight common crayon colors (red, blue, yellow, green, orange, purple, brown, black). Provide each child with a copy of a crayon pattern from page 56. Next, ask each child to predict which color will be the class favorite as you record responses on a chart. Then have each child personalize his pattern, color it with his favorite crayon shade, and then cut it out. Invite each student to attach his pattern to the appropriate column on the graph; then discuss the results. So—what's your students' favorite color of crayon?

## Shining Through

Here's a nifty small-group experiment that your little scientists won't be able to resist! In advance, gather a class supply of 12" x 18" construction paper and brightly colored crayons (fluorescent ones work well). Also mix up a batch of blue tempera paint thinned with water. You'll also need paintbrushes and a supply of paper towels.

Invite each youngster to fold a sheet of paper in half and then use crayons to lightly draw on one half of her paper. Next, direct her to bear down heavily as she draws more crayon pictures on the other half of the page. Invite each child to brush a thin wash of paint across her entire page, then wipe off any excess with a paper towel. Encourage youngsters to discuss the differences and similarities they see between the two halves of their paintings. Ask youngsters if they think the paint consistency affected the results. Then extend the experiment by inviting students to try various thicknesses of paint on more crayon resists.

### This Is Why

Crayons are made from pigments and liquid paraffin wax; wax resists water. The water-based tempera paint soaked into the construction paper, but not where the crayon was heavily colored. The paint was unable to penetrate the paper because the wax in the crayon resisted the paint.

## Earth Day Meltdown

Here's a grand way to celebrate Earth Day, or any day! To prepare, personalize a five-ounce paper cup for each child. Gather muffin tins, crayon shavings, and old peeled crayon pieces. Invite each child in a small group to place approximately one inch of crayon pieces and shavings into his cup, then place it into a muffin tin compartment. Place the tin in a 350-degree oven for approximately five minutes, or until the crayon pieces have just melted. Remove the tins from the oven and allow the crayon cups to cool completely. Then direct each child to peel the paper cup from his "new" crayon. If desired, conclude the activity by having students use their new crayons to draw step-by-step picture cards depicting how they made them. For an *extra* special Earth Day, why not make "earth" crayons by melting only blue and green crayon pieces and shavings?

### This Is Why

Crayons have a low melting point, which refers to the temperature at which a solid turns to liquid. When the melted crayons cool, they harden into a solid again.

## Home Learning Lab

Here's a colorful inquiry-based idea to involve families in student learning. Duplicate the report sheet on page 56 to make a class set. Encourage each youngster to take home her sheet and chart the favorite color of three different family members (or neighbors). After students have returned their sheets, discuss their findings. Encourage each child to look for similarities within her family's favorite colors; then challenge students to compare the overall findings. Hey—lots of people like blue!

## My Crayon

You can shave it, melt it, make rubbings with it…there are plenty of things to do with a crayon! Making this discovery booklet will be heaps of fun for little hands.

**For each booklet you will need:**
- a white construction paper copy of the booklet cover and pages (pages 52–55)
- scissors
- crayons
- plastic needlepoint mesh or burlap
- a handheld pencil sharpener
- glue
- two 8" x 2½" sheets of waxed paper
- an iron set on the lowest temperature (and an adult volunteer)
- thin tempera paint (any color)
- paintbrushes

**To make one booklet:**
Read the booklet aloud. Cut out the booklet cover and pages; then follow these suggestions to complete each page.

**Cover:** Color the crayon with your favorite color. Write your name on the line.

**Page 1:** Trace the line with your crayon.

**Page 2:** Color the page with the side of your crayon.

**Page 3:** Make a rubbing with your crayon.

**Page 4:** Using a handheld pencil sharpener, make a few crayon shavings. Glue them to the page.

**Page 5:** Make more crayon shavings. Sandwich them between two sheets of waxed paper; then have an adult iron them together. After the waxed paper has cooled, trim it and glue it to the page.

**Page 6:** Draw a picture using heavy strokes. Paint over your drawing with contrasting paint.

**Page 7:** Draw a picture of an object that is the same color as your crayon.

51

# Booklet Cover and Page 1
Use with "My Crayon" on page 51.

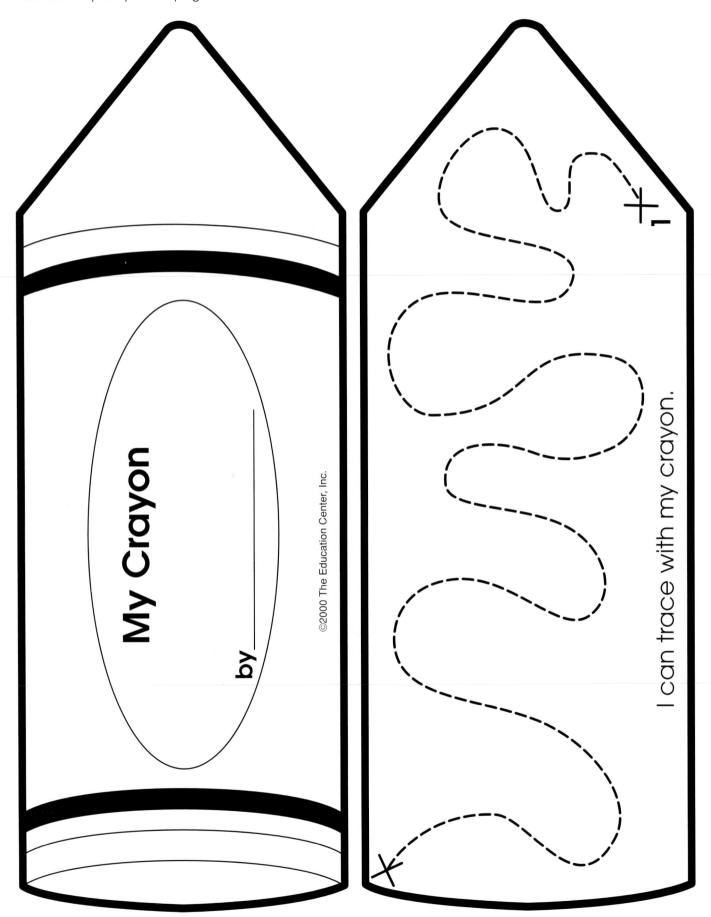

My Crayon

by _____

©2000 The Education Center, Inc.

I can trace with my crayon.

✗

✗
1

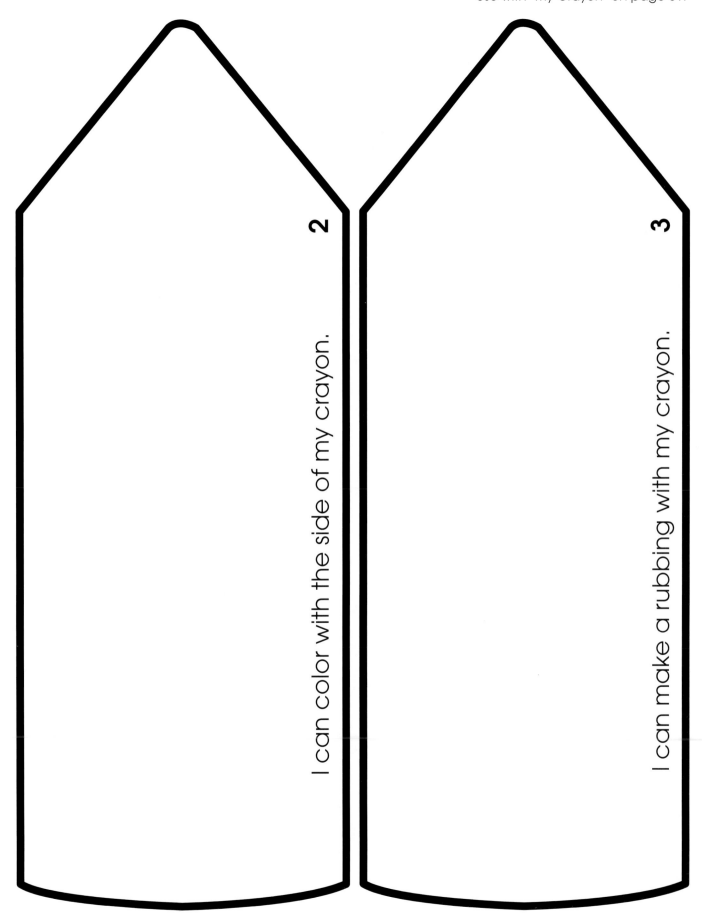

2

I can color with the side of my crayon.

3

I can make a rubbing with my crayon.

# Booklet Pages 4 and 5

Use with "My Crayon" on page 51.

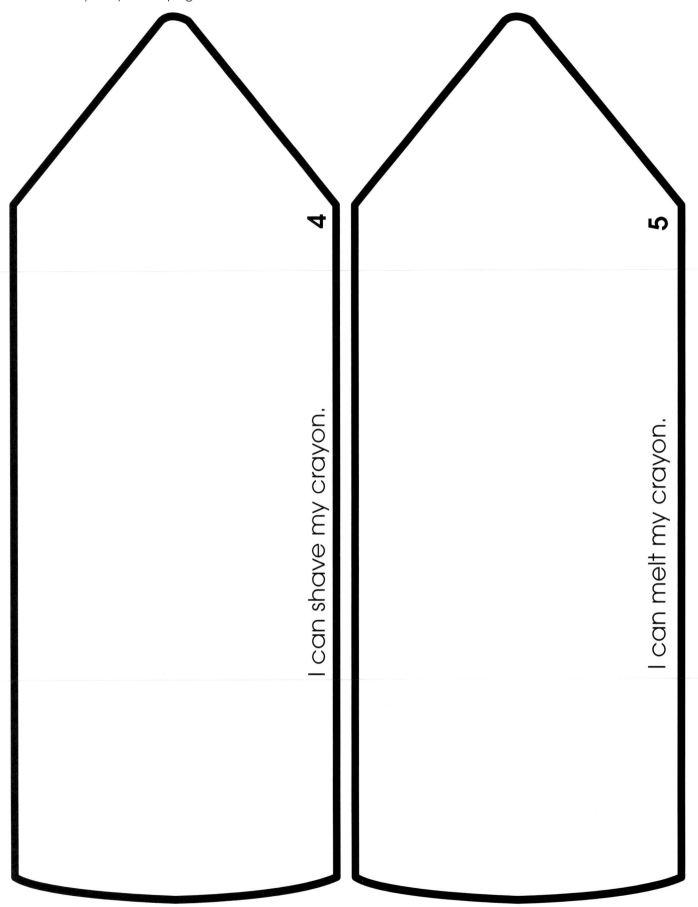

4

I can shave my crayon.

5

I can melt my crayon.

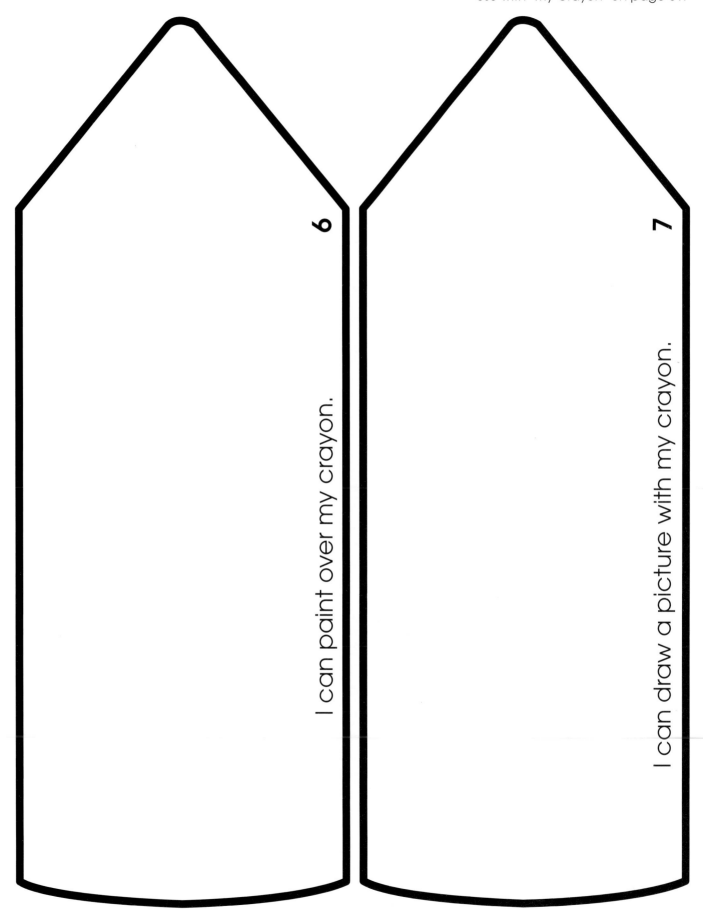

6

I can paint over my crayon.

7

I can draw a picture with my crayon.

# Home Learning Lab Report Sheet

Name _____

## Dear Parent,

We've been learning all about crayons and different ways they can be used. We've also noticed that there are many beautiful colors available. Please help your child survey three family members (or neighbors) to find out their favorite colors, and then complete a crayon (below) for each response.

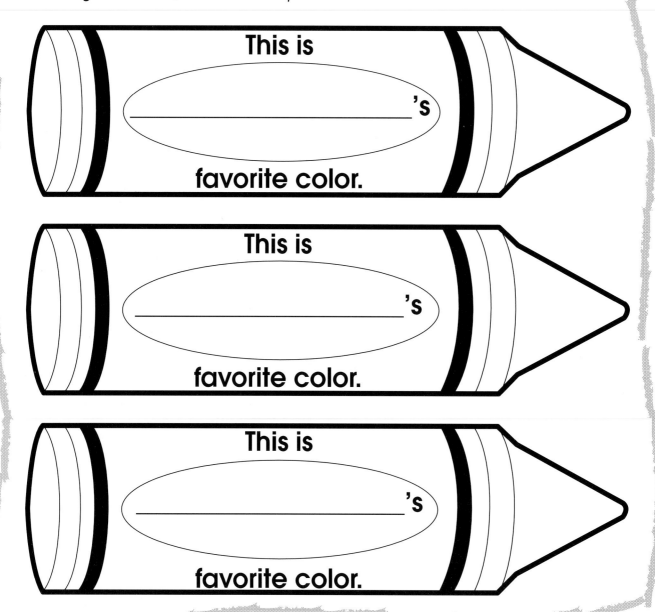

This is

_____'s

favorite color.

This is

_____'s

favorite color.

This is

_____'s

favorite color.

**Note to the teacher:** Use with "Home Learning Lab" on page 51. Also use the crayon pattern with "And the Winner Is…" on page 49.

# Healthful Habits Head to Toe

Get every body in tip-top shape with this introduction to good health habits.

## Good for Me

Here's a musical introduction to the topic of good health habits. Before teaching the following song to your students, ask them to identify some healthful habits. Guide them to include such things as exercising, getting a good night's sleep, staying clean, and eating nutritious foods. Jot their suggestions on a sheet of chart paper labeled "What's Good for Me?" Then teach little ones this song, substituting phrases from the chart for the underlined words each time you repeat the verse.

*(sung to the tune of "The Wheels on the Bus")*

[Healthful habits] are good for me,
Good for me, good for me.
[Healthful habits] are good for me
All day long!

**What's Good for Me?**

Eating vegtables      —Trisha
Drinking milk      —Piel
Going to bed on time      —Janae
Taking a nap      —Robert
Playing outside      —Ellie

## Home Learning Lab

Include parents in some habit-forming fun with this take-home activity. Send home a copy of page 61 with each child. Encourage him to work with his family each morning to record the number of hours he slept the previous night.

## Sleep Secrets

Big or little, young or old—everyone does it. What is it? Sleep! Share the following facts about sleep with your little ones. Then ask your students to share some ways they settle down before going to sleep. How about taking a bath? Reading a book? Or listening to music? Record each suggestion on a pastel-colored construction paper pillow shape. Display the pillow cutouts on a classroom wall. You may want to review these settling-down techniques (at least the ones that are classroom-appropriate) when rest time rolls around!

Listen to music

Take a bath

Read a book

**Sleep Facts**
- Sleep is a natural process that allows a person's body to rest and repair itself.
- Children need more sleep than adults.
- Most children between the ages of three and six sleep 10 to 12 hours each day.
- Our brains need sleep! Without sleep, people can become irritable and forget things easily.

## Wash Your Hands

This small-group activity is a handy way to demonstrate the basics of germ removal! In advance, gather an eyedropper for each child in a small group. You'll also need a pie pan filled with vegetable oil, two buckets of warm water, some liquid soap, and paper towels.

Invite each child in the group to fill his eyedropper with oil. Have him squirt the oil into the palm of one hand, then rub the oil over both hands. Explain that the oil is like germs. You get germs on your hands from many things that you touch throughout the day. How can your little ones get rid of these oil "germs"? By washing their hands! Bring out one of the buckets of warm water and ask each child to wash his hands *without* soap. Ask your youngsters if the oil "germs" are gone from their hands. Explain that germs can be washed away only if soap is used. Then bring out the second bucket of water and give each of your young scientists a squirt of liquid soap. Encourage youngsters to lather up and scrub for about 15 seconds.

## Don't Share Your Sneezes!

Ahhh-choo! Are students sneezing in your classroom? Seize this teachable moment and demonstrate to youngsters why sneezes shouldn't be shared. Bring a spray bottle of water to your group time. Spray some water on a sheet of colored construction paper as your group watches. Explain that when we sneeze, germs travel out of our mouths and noses and into the air for others to breathe. So if you share a sneeze, you're also sharing germs! Next, cover the spray bottle nozzle with a tissue and make the bottle "sneeze" into the tissue. Did the tissue stop the sneeze? You bet! Then give each child a chance to make the bottle "sneeze" into a fresh tissue. Wrap up this activity with a catchy tune to help youngsters remember how to put the freeze on the germs from a sneeze!

*(sung to the tune of "Pop! Goes the Weasel")*

When you feel a sneeze coming on,
You sure don't want to share it!
Grab a tissue as quick as you can.
DON'T share your sneezes!

## Smart Snacks

Teach your little ones to keep those good health habits going all day by choosing good-for-you snacks. First, ask students to brainstorm a list of snack foods as you write their ideas on a sheet of chart paper. Explain that eating a snack is a great way to get more energy and nutrients into your body. But it should be a smart snack! A smart snack helps your body get energy and nutrients, tastes good, and is low in fat, sugar, and salt. So what's the perfect smart snack? Fruit! Ask youngsters to brainstorm a list of fruits as you write their responses on another sheet of chart paper. Then ask each child to choose her favorite fruit from the list and illustrate it on a 12" x 18" sheet of white construction paper. Add a line of text to each child's drawing. Then stack all the pages between poster board covers and bind the book along the left side. Title this mouthwatering book "Smart Snacks" and decorate the cover with fruit stickers, perhaps scented ones. Add this yummy book to your class library.

AJ likes oranges for a snack.

## A Six-Pack Fruit Snack

Encourage your smart snackers to gobble up a variety of fresh fruit with this tasty activity. In advance, ask parents to donate prepared fresh fruits, such as cantaloupe chunks, seedless grapes, sliced strawberries, apple wedges, pear slices, pineapple chunks, orange or tangerine sections, and bananas (to prevent browning, peel and slice these just before the activity). Place each fruit in a separate serving bowl with a spoon. Gather a six-cup muffin tin for each child in a small group and purchase a package of cupcake liners.

Invite one small group of students at a time to your snack table. Give each child a muffin tin with cupcake liners in the cups. Encourage each child to place a spoonful of a different fruit into each of the six cups of her tin. Then invite everyone to snack on their six-pack fruit snack. Take a vote to decide on the group's favorite fruit. Did anyone try something new today? Congratulations, smart snackers!

## A Fresh and Fruity Booklet

Eating fruit is one healthful habit you don't want little ones to forget! So have them illustrate these booklets and take them home as reminders of this smart—and scrumptious—snack! Duplicate the booklet cover and text strips on page 62 for each child. Cut five 5" x 8" blank booklet pages per child. Read through the directions below and gather the necessary materials.

Working with one small group at a time, help students read through the text strips and then cut them apart. Direct each child to glue one strip to each of her blank booklet pages. Then have each child illustrate her pages according to the suggestions below. Later, help each student sequence the pages and then staple the booklet along the left side.

**Cover:** Write your name on the line. Draw and color different fruits.
**Page 1:** Make green tempera paint thumbprints.
**Page 2:** Glue on orange construction paper triangles.
**Page 3:** Cut heart shapes from red tissue paper. Glue them to the page; then use a correction pen or a toothpick dipped in yellow tempera paint to add "seeds."
**Page 4:** Sponge-paint watermelon chunks. When the paint is dry, use a thin black marker to add "seeds."
**Page 5:** Use markers to draw your favorite fruit; then write its name on the line.

I LIKE FRUIT!
by Demetria

I like to eat grapes   1
I like to eat cantaloupe   2
I like to eat strawberries   3
I like to eat watermelon   4
I like to eat pineapple   5

59

## The Safety Game

Being healthy means being safe, so use this variation on a classic game to review some good safety practices. Explain to your students that you are going to read a series of statements (see below) and that they must decide as a group whether each statement is safe or unsafe. If the group decides correctly, they will get one letter in the word *safety* written on the chalkboard. Once they've spelled the entire word, they'll get a reward, such as an extra ten minutes of *safe* play on the playground!

If desired, make this a team game. Divide your class into two teams and have the teams compete to see who can spell the word *safety* first. Add additional safety statements the next time you play to keep the game fresh.

- Always look both ways before crossing the street.
- It is OK to play in the street.
- Cross the street at a crosswalk.
- It is OK to play with matches.
- Cross the street without looking both ways.
- Remember your phone number and address.
- Don't talk to strangers.
- It's OK to ride a bike without a helmet.
- Keep your fingers away from electrical outlets.
- Always swim alone.
- You don't need to know your address.
- Stay with your family in a crowded place.
- Always buckle up in the car.

## Hip, Hip, Hooray for Helmets!

When it comes to healthful habits, wearing a helmet for sports activities is at the top of the list! Encourage all your students (and their parents) to wear helmets for biking and skating by holding a Helmet Day at school. Send home a note asking that students who have them bring their helmets to school. Bring in your own bicycle helmet and demonstrate the proper way to wear it. Inform students that the helmet should sit squarely on top of the head and cover the forehead. Help each child who has brought in her helmet to put it on properly. Then invite your helmeted youngsters to sing the following song to stress the importance of wearing helmets. Complete your Helmet Day activities by inviting youngsters to enjoy an extended playtime with your ride-on toys—wearing their helmets, of course!

*(sung to the tune of "If You're Happy and You Know It")*

Wear a helmet when you [bike]—put it on!
Wear a helmet when you [bike]—put it on!
If you have a little wreck,
Then your head it will protect!
Wear a helmet when you [bike]—put it on!

*Repeat the verse, substituting the word* skate *for the underlined word.*

# Power by the Hour

Dear Parent,

    Did you know that most children aged three to six sleep 12 hours each night? Each morning for the next few days, have your child color in one square for each hour of sleep received. Remember, each hour of sleep is an hour of power!

| Day 1 | Day 2 | Day 3 | Day 4 | Day 5 |
|:-----:|:-----:|:-----:|:-----:|:-----:|
| 12 | 12 | 12 | 12 | 12 |
| 11 | 11 | 11 | 11 | 11 |
| 10 | 10 | 10 | 10 | 10 |
| 9 | 9 | 9 | 9 | 9 |
| 8 | 8 | 8 | 8 | 8 |
| 7 | 7 | 7 | 7 | 7 |
| 6 | 6 | 6 | 6 | 6 |
| 5 | 5 | 5 | 5 | 5 |
| 4 | 4 | 4 | 4 | 4 |
| 3 | 3 | 3 | 3 | 3 |
| 2 | 2 | 2 | 2 | 2 |
| 1 | 1 | 1 | 1 | 1 |

# Booklet Cover and Text Strips
Use with "A Fresh and Fruity Booklet" on page 59.

# I LIKE FRUIT!

by _____

| | |
|---|---|
| I like to eat grapes. | 1 |
| I like to eat cantaloupe. | 2 |
| I like to eat strawberries. | 3 |
| I like to eat watermelon. | 4 |
| I like to eat _____. | 5 |

# Science Highlights

# Getting in Touch With Texture

Bumpy, furry, smooth—this texture unit is full of real feel appeal!

## That Certain Feeling

Touch base with textures as your youngsters feel their way through this hands-on investigation. In advance, fill a large feely bag or a pillowcase with a variety of textured items (see the list below for ideas). Label a set of cards with different texture words such as *soft, rough,* and *smooth.* Place the cards and bag in the center of your circle area.

Begin the activity by explaining to your group that each object in the bag has a particular type of feel, or *texture,* that our fingers recognize. Next, challenge your group to test their tactile abilities. Sing the song at right, naming both a child and texture where indicated. Invite that child to reach into the bag for the object. Then ask her to pair the object with its corresponding word card. Repeat the song several times with different students and textures. For more practice and fun, place the feely bag, texture items, and word cards in a center for pairs of students to further explore!

| Soft | Rough | Smooth |
|------|-------|--------|
| cotton balls | sandpaper | flat button |
| yarn | pinecone | plastic egg |
| towel | scrub pad | rubber eraser |
| stuffed animal | Styrofoam® ball | hard rubber ball |

*(sung to the tune of "Mary Had a Little Lamb")*

Can [child's name] find something [soft],
Something [soft], something [soft]?
Can [child's name] find something [soft]?
In our feely bag?
[Child's name] found something [soft],
Something [soft], something [soft].
[Child's name] found something [soft]
In our feely bag.

soft    rough    smooth

" Alex touched something soft. It was yarn."

## Picture That Feeling

Continue the feely fun with this picture-perfect display. In advance, program a sheet of paper with the sentences "_____ touched something _____. It was _____." Then duplicate it to make a class supply. Explain to youngsters that every object has a *texture* that they feel because of special touch receptors inside their fingers. Give each child a copy of the programmed sheet and ask him to write his name on the first blank line. Invite each child to draw a picture of something he discovered in the feely bag. Then help him complete the sentences as shown. Mount the finished texture pictures on a bulletin board titled "Picture That Feeling." Also mount small samples of the pictured texture objects for a truly textural display!

63

## Texture Treasures

Track down textures with this treasure hunt activity. To prepare, label a set of cards with texture words (or use the cards from "That Certain Feeling" on page 63) and then collect several lunch-size paper bags. Divide your youngsters into small groups and then give each group a texture word card and a bag. Instruct each group to fill their bag with items that match their assigned texture. Later, invite each group to share the items they have collected; then challenge classmates to guess the group's texture word. Now, that's textural treasure!

### Did You Know?

Our skin helps us collect information. When we touch something, our skin detects whether it is rough, smooth, or bumpy. Skin contains *nerve endings* that send messages about touch to our brains.

rough

## The Eyes Have It

Focus your youngsters' attention on sight as a way to describe textures with this sensory activity. Share the wordless book *Is It Rough? Is It Smooth? Is It Shiny?* by Tana Hoban (Greenwillow Books) with your children. Encourage youngsters to carefully observe the photographs on each page; then discuss how each pictured object may *feel* to the touch. Explain to students that shiny objects are slick, or smooth-textured enough to reflect light. Next, ask youngsters to describe the textures. Record their responses on a chart as shown. Extend this activity by showing youngsters a variety of textured objects and having them guess how each one might feel. Then invite youngsters to touch each object to determine whether their hypothesis was correct. What a smooth idea!

| rough | smooth |
|---|---|
| elephant skin rocks | apples pennies (shiny, too) eggs star wand (shiny, too) |

## Art With Feeling

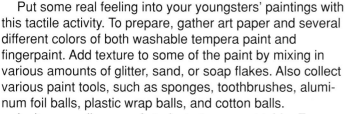

Put some real feeling into your youngsters' paintings with this tactile activity. To prepare, gather art paper and several different colors of both washable tempera paint and fingerpaint. Add texture to some of the paint by mixing in various amounts of glitter, sand, or soap flakes. Also collect various paint tools, such as sponges, toothbrushes, aluminum foil balls, plastic wrap balls, and cotton balls.

Invite a small group of students to your art table. Encourage each child to experiment with the different paints, tools, and, of course, their fingers! As the children are painting, discuss the many textures in the paint and the effects made by their fingers and the tools. Bet they'll have lots to say about this touchy-feely art!

## Touchable Portraits

Youngsters will enjoy putting the finishing touches on self-portraits with this imaginative art idea. To prepare, collect one sturdy paper plate for each child, a hand mirror, white glue, a construction paper conversation balloon, and various textured art supplies (see the list below for suggestions). Ask each child in a small group to observe himself in the mirror. Then give him a paper plate and guide him as he uses the textural supplies to create a stunning self-portrait. When the portraits are dry, display each one with a personalized conversation balloon as shown. Darling, you look fabulous!

I have fuzzy orange ears.

**Textured art supplies:**

| | | |
|---|---|---|
| faux fur | foil | waxed paper |
| pipe cleaners | felt | wiggle eyes |
| fabric | feathers | pom-poms |
| sandpaper | craft foam | crepe paper |
| yarn | cotton balls | crinkle strips |
| buttons | tissue | bubble wrap |

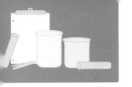

## Ready, Set, Rub!

Buff up fine-motor skills with this texture rubbing activity. In advance, create texture templates by drawing a different shape on each of several poster board squares with a thick line of glue (for colorful templates, tint the glue with tempera paint) as shown. Let the templates dry overnight; then securely tape each one to a tabletop (or similar surface) in your art center. Model the process of texture rubbing for your youngsters. Give a small group of children several sheets of white paper, crayons, colored pencils, and markers; then encourage them to experiment and create different rubbings. Extend the activity by inviting each child to mount her favorite rubbing on a folded sheet of construction paper to make a personalized card for a loved one.

## Texture Rubbings Booklet

Are your little ones ready to try some independent rubbings? Then have them make these booklets. In advance, copy the booklet cover on page 68 to make a class set. Next, assemble a rubbings tool kit for each child by placing several 4 1/2" x 7" sheets of copy paper, a peeled crayon, and a sharp pencil into a resealable plastic bag. Divide youngsters into small groups and give each child her tool kit. Instruct each group to search for textured surfaces to make a different rubbing on each sheet, such as floor tile, a brick wall, a sidewalk, a leaf, etc. Assist each youngster in writing the object name on each rubbing sheet. Later, give each child a booklet cover to personalize and color. Then help each child stack all her pages behind the cover and staple them together along the left side. Encourage youngsters to take their texture booklets home to read to their family. What a neat way to keep in touch!

## Home Learning Lab

Now that your little ones have had some experience making texture rubbings, encourage them to experiment with other surfaces at home. Duplicate page 69 to make a class supply, and send home one sheet with each child. Later, as each child shares her homemade rubbings, challenge students to guess each object.

## Tactile Match

Feel the excitement as your little matchmakers play this center game. To prepare, use paper and crayons to create rubbings of several common classroom and household items, such as a comb, puzzle pieces, a ruler, safety scissors, etc. Then place the real objects and the rubbing sheets at the center. Invite a small group of youngsters to match each real object with its rubbed representation. How perceptive!

# What Has Texture?

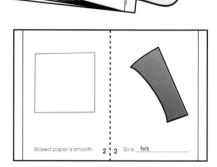

There are plenty of reading skills woven into this little touchy-feely booklet. To prepare, duplicate the booklet pages (70–72) to make a class supply, and then cut a 7 1/2" x 5" piece of poster board for each child. Next, gather for each child a cotton ball and a two-inch square of each of the following materials: sandpaper, waxed paper, and bubble wrap. You will also need a variety of rough, smooth, bumpy, and soft items for each child to choose from to complete her booklet (see the suggestion list for "Touchable Portraits" on page 65).

To make a booklet, cut apart the pages and then glue page 5 onto the piece of poster board. Sequence each set of pages behind the appropriate cover, and then staple both sets to page 5 as shown. Read the booklet aloud and then help each child complete her booklet according to the suggestions below. Your youngsters will master the repetitive context clues as they read—and feel—this booklet again and again!

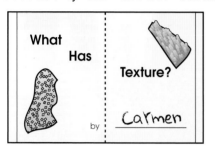

**Cover:** Write your name on the line. Glue on two different-textured items.

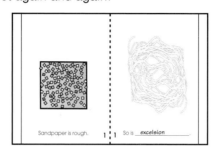

**Page 1:** Glue a square of sandpaper on the left side. Glue a rough material on the right side, and then write its name on the line.

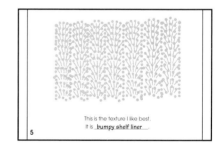

**Page 2:** Glue a square of waxed paper on the left side. Glue a smooth material on the right side, and then write its name on the line.

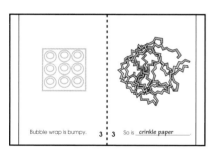

**Page 3:** Glue a square of bubble wrap on the left side. Glue a bumpy material on the right side, and then write its name on the line.

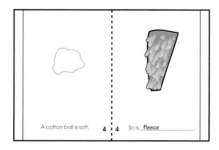

**Page 4:** Glue a cotton ball on the left side. Glue a soft material on the right side, and then write its name on the line.

**Page 5:** Glue a piece of your favorite textured material to the center of the page. Write its name on the line.

# Sticky, Smooth, Hard (and Sweet!)

Culminate this unit by helping your little ones get their just desserts! Serve each child an ice-cream sundae that's chock-full of different textures. Begin with a smooth scoop of ice cream covered in sticky chocolate syrup. Add some hard chopped nuts, bumpy nonpareils, soft mini marshmallows, and a chewy cherry. Now, that's a tasty way to make sure students get the scoop on texture!

My

Texture Rubbings

Booklet

by

_____

©2000 The Education Center, Inc. • *Science for All Seasons* • *Spring* • TEC3049

My

Texture Rubbings

Booklet

by

_____

©2000 The Education Center, Inc. • *Science for All Seasons* • *Spring* • TEC3049

# Time for a Texture Hunt

Dear Parent,

   We have been studying textures and exploring objects that are rough, smooth, soft, and bumpy. We have learned how to make rubbings of different textures. Please help your child go on a texture hunt, searching for two different textures to make rubbings in the boxes below. Then help your child write the name of each object. Please return this sheet by _____ so we can share them at school. Rub-a-dub-dub!

This is a _____.

This is a _____.

©2000 The Education Center, Inc. • *Science for All Seasons* • *Spring* • TEC3049

# What Has

Texture?

by _____

*• Science for All Seasons • Spring •* TEC3049

Sandpaper is rough.

So is _____.

**1**   1

Waxed paper is smooth.

So is _____.

**2**  **2**

Bubble wrap is bumpy.

So is _____.

**3**  **3**

A cotton ball is soft.

So is _____.

**4** **4**

This is the texture I like best.
It is _____.

**5**

# Wet Detectives

Splash! Soak up plenty of water absorption and repellency knowledge with this investigative unit.

## Hide and Seek

Rev up your science sleuths' observation and communication skills with this introductory look at absorption. Begin by passing a large, fat, dry sponge (such as a car wash sponge) around your circle; then ask students what they think will happen if water is poured over the sponge. Incorporate the definition of the word *absorb* (to suck up or take up) into the discussion. Then perform this experiment to determine whether the sponge will suck up the water. Gather youngsters around and place the sponge on a tray. Have students carefully observe as you slowly pour a half cup of water over the sponge. Encourage your group to watch the tray for signs of water, and challenge them to explain where the water is hiding. Then ask a volunteer to squeeze the sponge, releasing the water onto the tray. So that's where the water was hiding!

Next, compare another object's absorption ability with that of the sponge. Place a large wooden block (from your block center) on the tray. Have students predict what will happen; then repeat the experiment, encouraging youngsters to carefully observe the block and tray for telltale signs of water. What happened this time?

## This Is Why

The sponge is *porous,* which means it has many holes in it. When the sponge comes in contact with water, the holes fill with water. The block has no holes to fill, so the water does not soak in.

## Soak It Up!

Youngsters will absorb lots of science in this inquiry-based center! Stock a center with eyedroppers, a shallow dish of water, test items (see the list below for suggestions), a muffin tin for each child in the center, and a supply of paper towels. Begin by asking a small group of children to predict which objects will absorb water. Then invite each little investigator to select several items that she would like to test for absorbency. Have her place one item in each section of her muffin tin; then use the eyedropper to squirt water on each of them. Which items soak up the water? After each student has had a chance to explore, encourage the group to discuss the results. Now, there's an activity that's dripping with good, clean fun!

**Try These!**

| | |
|---|---|
| foil | scissors |
| facial tissue | marbles |
| shells | paper towels |
| pom-poms | blocks |
| yarn | cloth |
| pencil | plastic lids |
| pebbles | cotton balls |
| sponge | squares cut from a plastic |
| waxed paper | shower liner or curtain |

## Towel Test

After testing the materials in "Soak It Up!" (page 73), your little ones will know that paper towels absorb water. But which brand of paper towel absorbs the most water? Try this activity and find out!

Purchase three different brands of paper towels. Ask each of your little ones to predict which brand will soak up the most water, and jot their responses on chart paper. Place one sheet of each brand of paper towel on a separate tray or brownie pan. Begin the experiment by inviting volunteers to pour one tablespoon of water on each paper towel. Prompt students to carefully watch each tray for water. If the paper towels absorb the water, then invite more volunteers to pour another tablespoon of water on each of the paper towels. Continue the experiment until water begins to seep out of two of the paper towels, thereby determining the most absorbent towel. Be sure to tally the number of tablespoons of water used!

## What Would You Wear in the Rain?

Now that your little water specialists have had some experience testing materials for absorbency, they're probably asking about its natural opposite: repellency. Turn youngsters' attention to rain gear, and use this experiment to determine what types of materials are suitable for rain gear. In advance, gather a sponge, cotton cloth, wool fabric, a piece of vinyl tablecloth, and a container of water. Hold up the sponge and sing this song to the tune of "For He's a Jolly Good Fellow":

Oh, what would you wear in the rain?
What would you wear in the rain?
What would you wear in the rain?
Would you wear [a sponge]?

Would you wear [a sponge]?
Would you wear [a sponge]?

What would you wear in the rain?
What would you wear in the rain?
What would you wear in the rain?
Would you wear [a sponge]?

Pour some water on the sponge. Would a raincoat made of sponges keep you dry? Continue singing and testing each piece of material, substituting the underlined words with *some cotton, some wool,* and *some vinyl.* Discuss with students the desirability of using each of the materials to make an effective raincoat. Lead youngsters to conclude that water-repellent materials work best.

## What Will Keep Me Dry?

Here's a booklet that will certainly make a splash among your young scientists. To prepare, duplicate pages 76–78 for each of your students. Gather a class supply of the materials needed below. Have each child cut out booklet pages 1–4 and then follow the directions below to complete each page. Have each child sequence his pages and staple them to the top of the backing page. Encourage students to read each other's umbrella books. Then send the booklets home to be shared with family members. We know what will keep us dry!

**Backing page:** Color the umbrella handle. Glue a six-inch half circle of vinyl (use an old picnic tablecloth) or plastic shower liner to the top of the umbrella. Write your name on the line.

**Page 1:** Glue a six-inch half circle of tissue paper or paper towel to the top of the umbrella.

**Page 2:** Glue cotton balls to the top of the umbrella.

**Page 3:** Glue a six-inch half circle of cotton cloth or flannel to the top of the umbrella.

**Page 4:** Glue lengths of yarn to the top of the umbrella.

## Apple Action

Wrap up this unit in a lip-smacking way. Pass some dried apples (or other dried fruits) around your circle. Invite each of your little ones to sample a small portion. Encourage your science buffs to describe the way the dried apples look, feel, smell, and taste; record student comments on one side of an apple-shaped chart. Then reconstitute enough dried fruit for each child to have a taste by soaking it in water (in the refrigerator) overnight. The next day, give each child a portion of reconstituted apples. After each child has observed the fruit, record her descriptions of how it looks, feels, and smells. Finally, have her taste the reconstituted apples to determine whether they taste different, too.

### This Is Why

The dried apples have had all the water removed from them. When they were placed in water, the fruits absorbed the water they were missing.

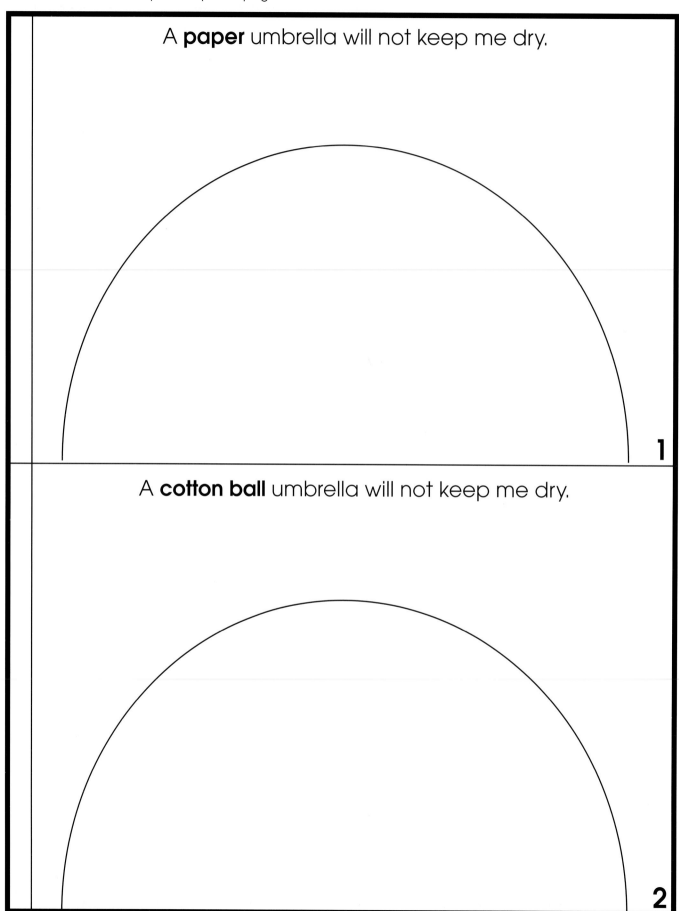

A **paper** umbrella will not keep me dry.

**1**

A **cotton ball** umbrella will not keep me dry.

**2**

A **cloth** umbrella will not keep me dry.

**3**

A **yarn** umbrella will not keep me dry.

**4**

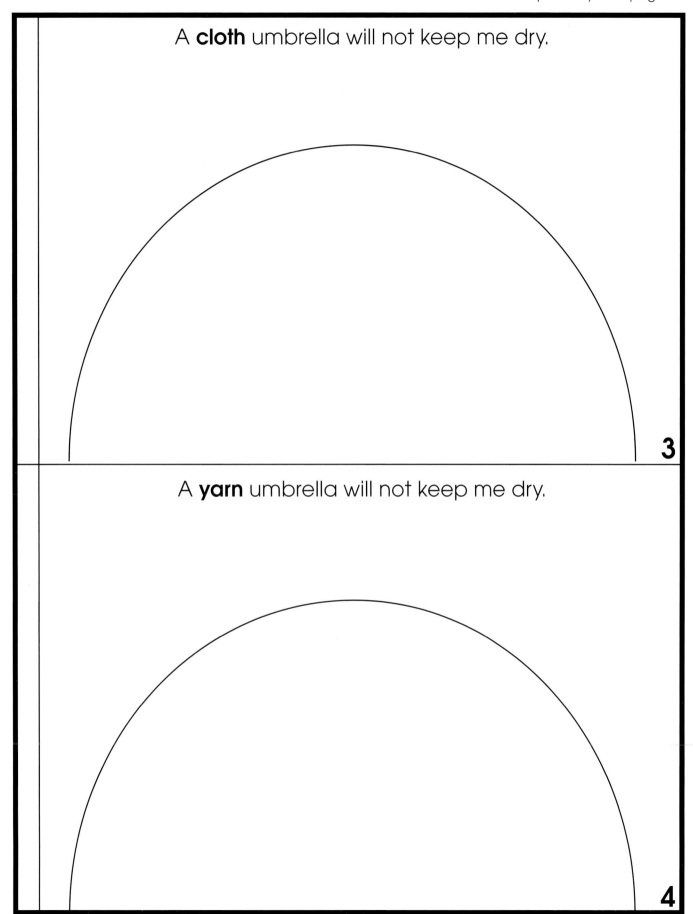

# Booklet Backing Page

Use with "What Will Keep Me Dry?" on page 75.

Here's an umbrella that will keep me dry!

# What Will Keep Me Dry?

by

_____

# The Word on Birds

The word is out—birds are some of the most interesting critters around! No matter where you live, your fledgling bird-watchers should be able to spy some of our most common feathered friends. So come on and wing into spring!

## Recognizing Robins

Introduce your bird study by inviting students to make the acquaintance of a fine-feathered mystery guest! Duplicate the robin pattern on page 83 on white construction paper. Color the wing, tail, head, and back of the robin's body brown. Color the breast red, the beak yellow, and the legs gray. Leave the throat white. Then cut out all the pieces and prepare them for use on your flannelboard. (Be sure to glue felt to the robin's body where you want to attach the wing and tail.)

At a group time, recite the rhyme below, pausing at the end of each line for students' guesses. Once students have guessed that the mystery visitor is a bird, put the robin together on your flannelboard. Ask youngsters to name the bird's body parts as you go. Then introduce your new bird friend as a robin. Tell your students that many people consider the appearance of robins on their lawn as a sure sign that spring has arrived!

A mystery guest is here today. It is a living thing.
It has two legs. It has two eyes. It really likes to sing!
It has a tail. It has a beak. It flaps two wings to fly.
Sometimes it hops across the grass. Sometimes it's in the sky.

## Hopping Robin Puppets

Now that your little ones know what a robin looks like, encourage them to put together their own robin puppets. Duplicate the robin pattern on page 83 on white construction paper to make a class supply. Have each child use your flannelboard robin as a guide for coloring the parts of her puppet. Then help her cut out the pieces and attach the wing, tail, and beak to the robin's body with brads. Have her glue the puppet to a wide craft stick. Then get those robins hoppin' to the following tune!

*(sung to the tune of "Bingo")*

The robin hops across the lawn. It's looking for a worm, oh!
R-O-B-I-N, R-O-B-I-N, R-O-B-I-N.
The robin [flicks her tail], oh!     *Move the puppet's tail up and down.*

*Repeat the verse two more times, substituting the following phrases and motions:*
flaps its wing...                    *Move the puppet's wing up and down.*
moves its beak...                    *Open and close the puppet's beak.*

# We're Going on a Worm Hunt

Why does a robin spend the morning hopping across the grass? It's catching wiggly worms for breakfast! Invite your youngsters to imitate robins when they go on a worm hunt of their own. To prepare this activity that will challenge your students' observation skills, cut ten 2-inch pieces each of brown, white, and green yarn. Scatter the yarn pieces on a grassy area outdoors. Then ask students to imagine they are hungry, sharp-eyed robins. Tell them they'll be hunting for brown, white, and green yarn "worms" outside. Then take them to the prepared hunting ground and set them loose as you sing this song to the tune of "London Bridge."

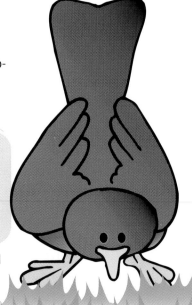

> Hungry robins look for worms, look for worms, look for worms.
> Hungry robins look for worms in the green grass.
>
> Hungry robins find some worms, find some worms, find some worms.
> Hungry robins find some worms in the green grass.

After you've sung both verses of the song, have students stop their search and head indoors, even if they've left some worms behind. Then continue with the graphing activity described below.

| brown | white | green |
|-------|-------|-------|

## Graphing the Catch

Have students tally their worm totals from "We're Going on a Worm Hunt" on a three-column graph labeled as shown. Have each student use tape to attach her yarn worms in the appropriate columns. Then discuss the results. Of which color do your robins have the most worms? The fewest? Which color was easiest to see in the grass? Which color of worms was the hardest to spot? Guide students to understand that the coloring of real worms and bugs can help to protect them from predators. Share the information in "This Is Why" with your young scientists.

### This Is Why

Coloration that helps an animal hide from predators is called *camouflage*. If an animal such as a worm has coloring similar to its environment, it is harder to see and can avoid being caught and eaten.

## The Best Beak

Birds use their beaks to pick up those fat, wriggly worms—and other types of food as well. Help your little ones discover more about birds' beaks with this comparison activity. Gather a class supply of paper plates, craft sticks, spring-type clothespins, and Gummy Worms® candies. Working with one small group at a time, place a candy worm on each child's plate; then give her a craft stick. Ask the child to try picking up the worm using *only* the craft stick. Have little ones discuss this type of worm-catching tool. Then have them compare their craft sticks with a bird's beak. Next, bring out the clothespins and have youngsters predict how well this type of beak might work. Invite each child to try picking up her worm with a clothespin. Once you've discussed the results, give your little birds the go-ahead to gobble those worms!

## Feathers Are Special

Just as birds' beaks are unique, so are their feathers. To inspire a brief study of feathers, give each child a craft feather to lay on her hand. Ask the child to decide if the feather is heavy or light. Lead little ones to understand that feathers' light weight makes them an ideal covering for flying creatures. To demonstrate, cut a sheet of construction paper in half to create two rectangular "wings." Have students work together to glue feathers to one wing and craft sticks to the other. Once the glue has dried, ask a student volunteer to hold one wing in each hand and stretch his arms out to his sides. Have him flap the wings and describe the effort involved on each side. Invite each child to take a turn flapping these wings so he can feel for himself why feathers are better for flying!

## Building a Bird

Now that your young scientists know about the unique features of birds, encourage each of them to draw a portrait of a feathered friend. Give each child a sheet of white construction paper and a pencil. Read the following poem as you guide youngsters to draw a bird, step-by-step. Later, have each child glue craft feathers or feather shapes cut from collage materials to the different parts of her drawing.

First an oval,

Then a circle on top,

Attach two legs so the bird can hop.

Draw a beak;

Add a tail and an eye.

Draw two wings. Now your bird can fly!

# Birds, Birds, Birds!

How many different types of birds can your youngsters name? Challenge them to brainstorm a list of all the bird names they know as you record them on chart paper. Then gather bird books from your library so that your young investigators can learn about even *more* birds! Place the books in a center, along with your chart, some bird posters, nature magazines that feature birds, and any other bird-themed items you can find. Here's a brief booklist to get you started:

*About Birds: A Guide for Children*
By John and Cathryn P. Sill
Published by Peachtree Publishers

*Amazing Birds* (Eyewitness Juniors)
By Alexandra Parsons
Published by Alfred A. Knopf, Inc.

*The Bird Alphabet Book*
By Jerry Pallotta
Published by Charlesbridge Publishing, Inc.

*Crinkleroot's Guide to Knowing the Birds*
By Jim Arnosky
Published by Aladdin Paperbacks

## All About Birds

Little ones will flock to complete these unique bird booklets! To prepare, duplicate pages 84–89 on white construction paper for each child. Have each child cut out a magazine picture of a favorite bird and glue it to the right cover (or have him draw a favorite bird). Then direct him to cut out the covers and write his name on the line. Next, ask each child to color and cut out the left and right halves of booklet pages 1 through 4. Then have him glue a few craft feathers to the center of booklet page 5 before cutting it out. To assemble his booklet, help the child stack his left and right pages and covers in order on top of page 5; then staple the booklet together along the sides.

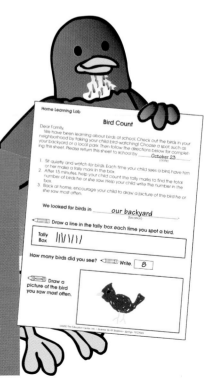

## Home Learning Lab

Send your fledgling scientists home with an activity that is sure to turn parent and child into eager bird-watching partners! Simply send home a copy of page 90 with each child. When the completed sheets have been returned to school, use them for one or more of the following data interpretation activities:

• Have students list all of the bird-watching locations that were selected. Which was the most popular?
• Graph the total number of birds each child sighted. Have students use the graph to find the greatest and fewest number of birds sighted. What was the most common number of birds sighted?
• Ask students to predict which kind of bird was most often sighted. Using the lab sheets, make a tally of the different types of birds to check their predictions.

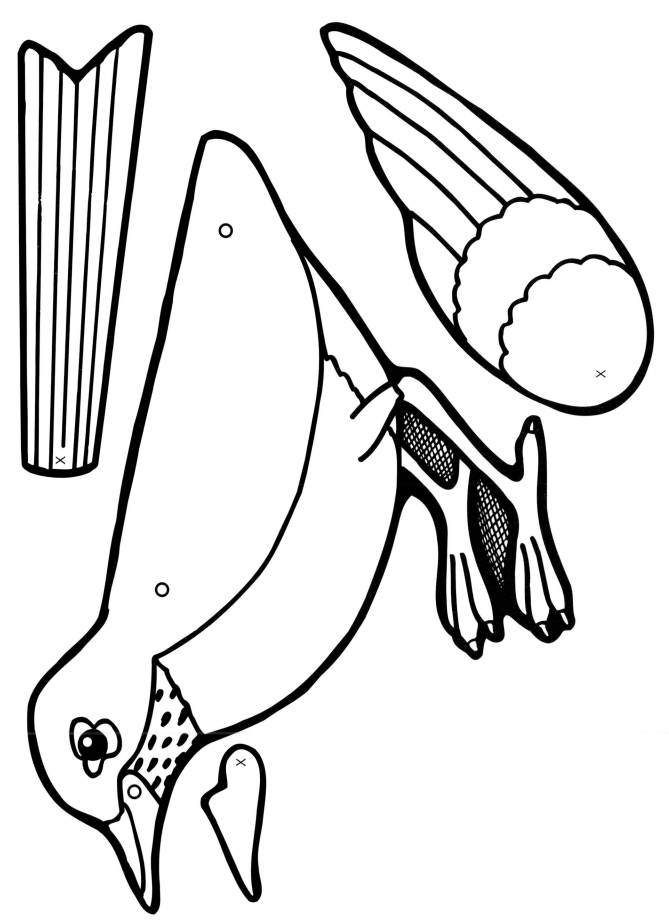

# Left and Right Booklet Covers
Use with "All About Birds" on page 82.

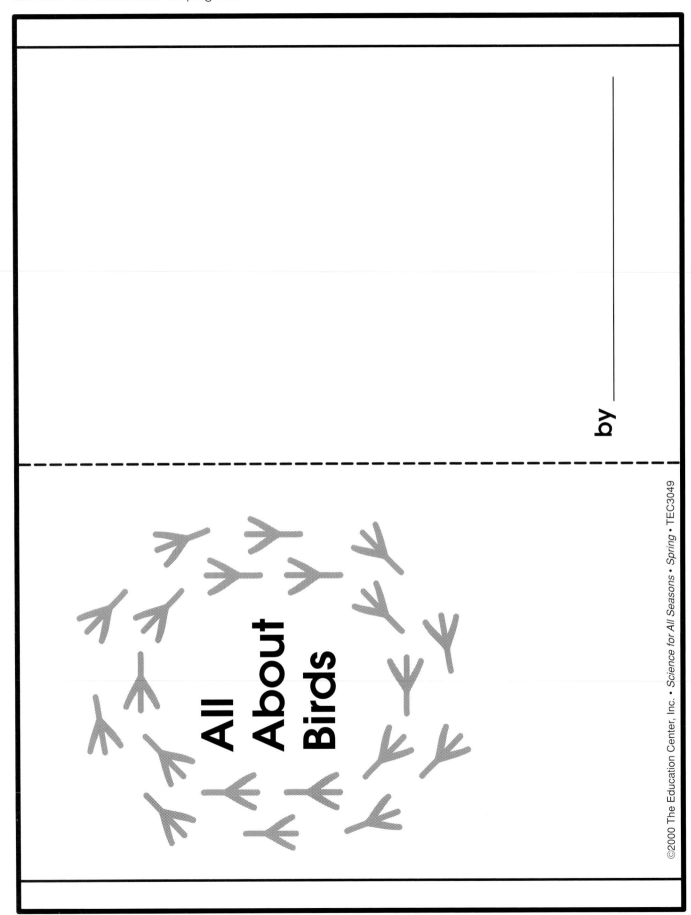

by _____

All About Birds

©2000 The Education Center, Inc. • *Science for All Seasons* • *Spring* • TEC3049

©2000 The Education Center, Inc. • *Science for All Seasons* • *Spring* • TEC3049

Some birds are **small**.

hummingbird

Some birds are **big**.

ostrich

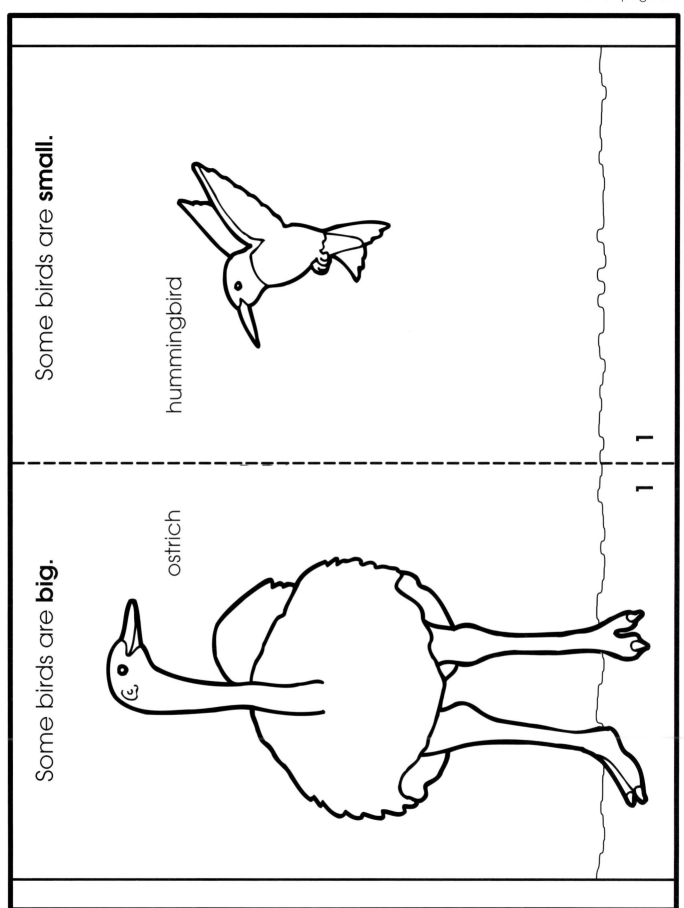

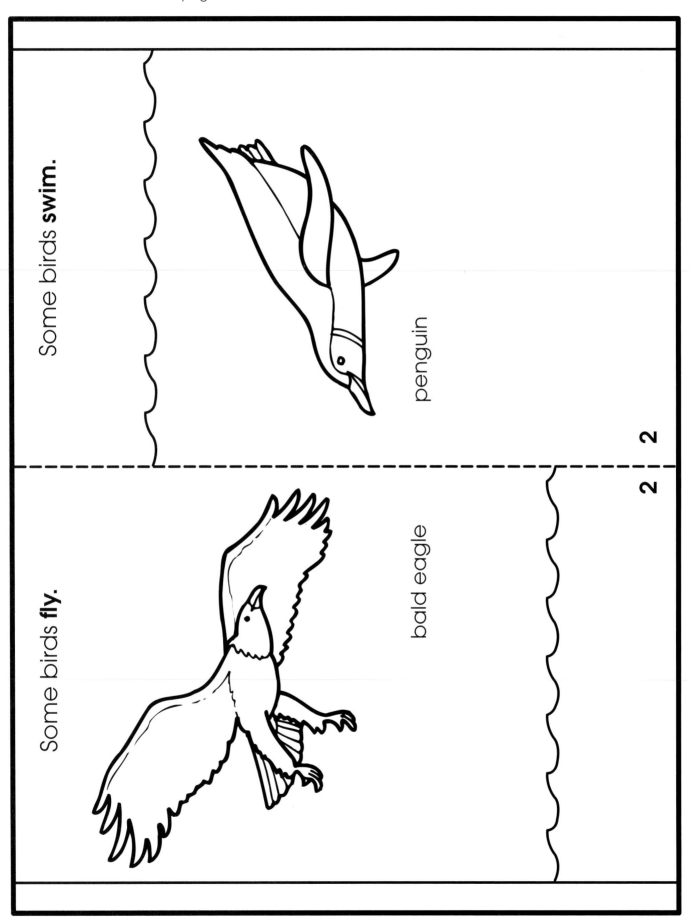

Some birds **swim**.

penguin

Some birds **fly**.

bald eagle

2 2

2

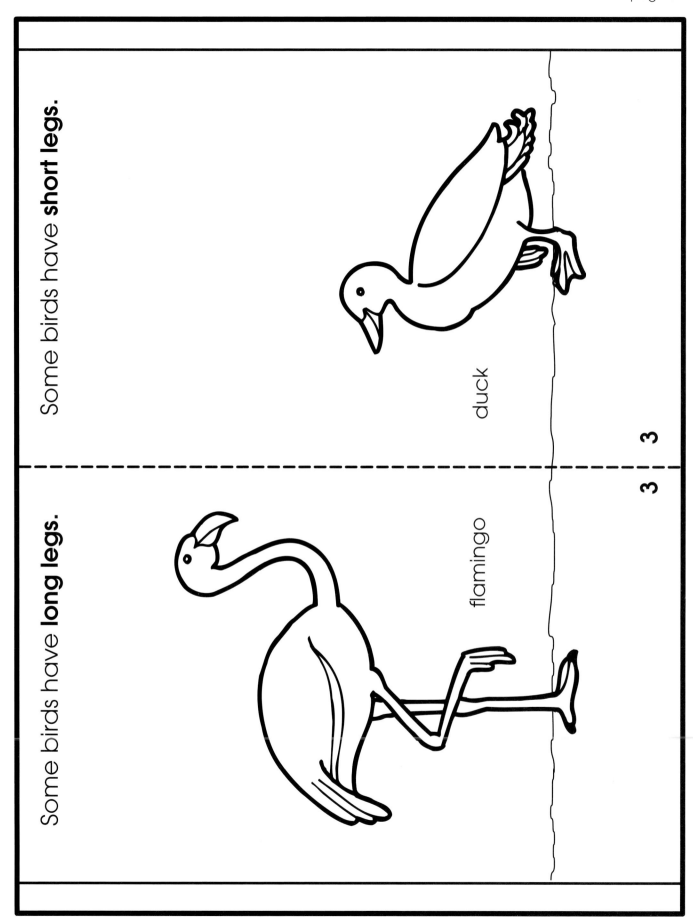

Some birds have **short legs.**

duck

Some birds have **long legs.**

flamingo

3    3

3

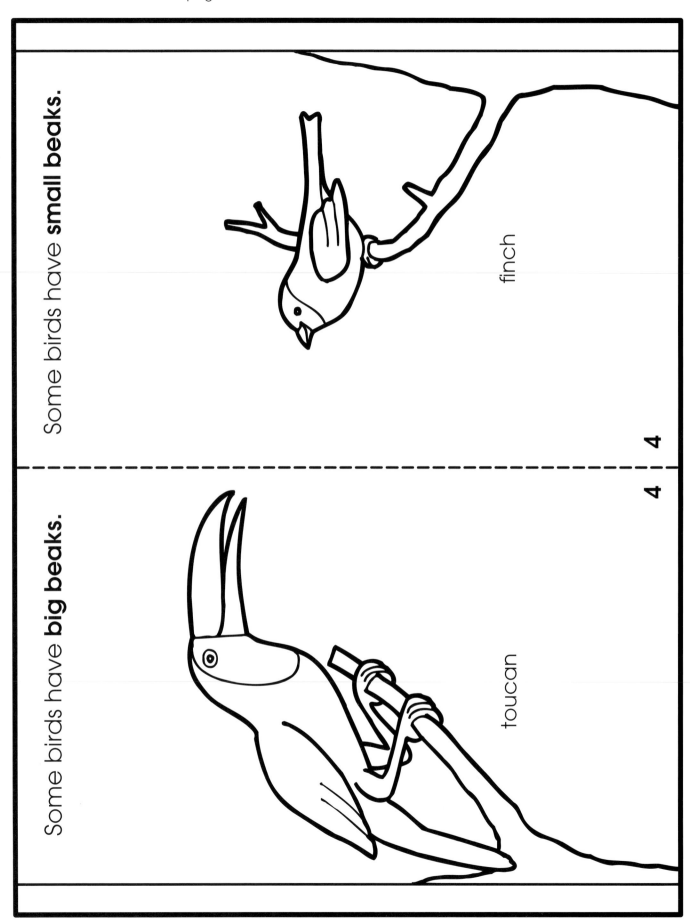

Some birds have **small beaks.**

finch

Some birds have **big beaks.**

toucan

4

4
4

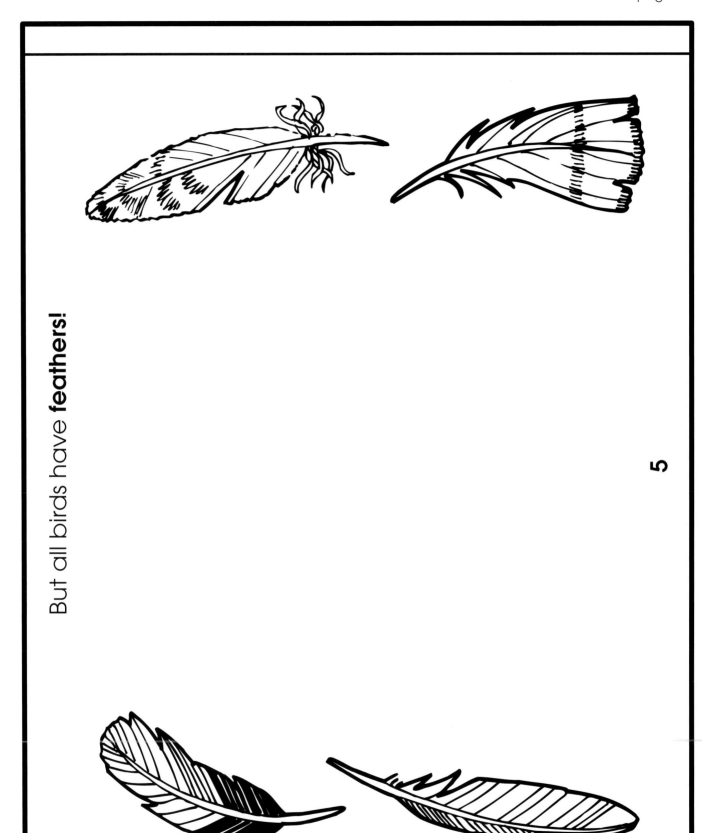

But all birds have **feathers!**

5

# Bird Count

Dear Family,
    We have been learning about birds at school. Check out the birds in your neighborhood by taking your child bird-watching! Choose a spot, such as your backyard or a local park. Then follow the directions below for completing this sheet. Please return this sheet to school by _____.
(date)

1. Sit quietly and watch for birds. Each time your child sees a bird, have him or her make a tally mark in the box.
2. After 15 minutes, help your child count the tally marks to find the total number of birds he or she saw. Help your child write the number in the box.
3. Back at home, encourage your child to draw a picture of the bird he or she saw most often.

**We looked for birds in** _____.
(location)

**Draw a line in the tally box each time you spot a bird.**

| Tally Box |
|---|
|  |

**How many birds did you see?** **Write.** [ ]

**Draw a picture of the bird you saw most often.**

©2000 The Education Center, Inc. • *Science for All Seasons* • *Spring* • TEC3049

**Note to the teacher:** Use with "Home Learning Lab" on page 82.

# Bubbles, Bubbles Everywhere!

These discovery ideas will have your youngsters bursting with excitement for bubbleology—the science of bubbles!

## Whisked Away by Bubbles

Introduce your little ones to sudsy bubbles with this small-group activity. In advance, have a parent donate a bottle of clear dishwashing liquid. Half-fill your sensory table with water; then place several wire whisks (or rotary eggbeaters) nearby. Ask your students to predict whether bubbles can be made with plain water; then invite them to use the whisks to find out. Students will conclude that something else is needed to produce bubbles. Next, tell students that you have a magic bubble solution. Dramatically squirt some dishwashing liquid into the water. Then ask each child to predict what will happen when they use the whisks in the water this time. With just a flick of the wrist, your youngsters will see bunches and bunches of bubbles!

## This Is Why

A bubble is air that is trapped inside a liquid. Water does not produce bubbles because its molecules cling to each other, causing *surface tension*. Adding soap to the water weakens the surface tension and makes the water stretchy enough to form a bubble.

## Billions of Bright Bubbles!

Involve your little ones in making different-colored bubble mixtures for future outdoor use! Follow the recipe below to help your students make several batches. For best results, let the mixtures sit for at least five days before using. Before the bubble-blowing event, ask your students to predict whether the added food coloring will affect the color of the bubbles. Then invite your little learners to blow as many bubbles as they can. Oooh—bright bubbles!

## Home Learning Lab

Strengthen the home-school connection by having students and their families experiment with all kinds of bubble blowers! Send a copy of page 96 home with each student. Encourage your bubble scientists to have a big outdoor bubble blowout. Bubbles away!

**Bright Bubbles**
5 tbsp. soft water (or use distilled water)
4 tbsp. clear Dawn® dishwashing liquid
1 tbsp. light corn syrup
5 drops food coloring

## Stir Up Some Syrup Solution!

Pop! Bubbles don't tend to stay around very long. Involve your little scientists in discovering longer-lasting bubbles with this fun activity. In advance, make two batches of bubble solution by mixing five tablespoons of water with four tablespoons of Dawn® dish detergent in separate plastic containers. Add one tablespoon of light corn syrup to one of the mixtures; then label the container. Gather several bubble wands or make pipe cleaner wands similar to the one shown. Ask a group of students to brainstorm reasons bubbles burst so quickly. Then invite each child to blow a bubble from the first mixture and count how many seconds until the bubble pops. Have him repeat the activity with the corn syrup mixture. After comparing, your little ones will conclude that syrup is the solution to stronger bubbles!

One, two, three, four, ...

Corn Syrup

## This Is Why

Bubbles pop because the soapy solution dries, releasing the air inside them. Adding corn syrup (or glycerine) helps the bubbles hold more water, which makes them stronger.

**Bubble Paint Solution**
1/2 c. water
1/4 c. Dawn® dishwashing liquid
2 tsp. of tempera paint

## "Bubble-fly" Art

Your students will be bubbling over with enthusiasm when they make these lasting impressions of bubbles! In advance, enlarge, if desired, and duplicate the butterfly pattern on page 95 for each child. Gather a class supply of drinking straws and pipe cleaners. Then use the recipe below to make several colored bubble solutions, each in a separate yogurt cup. To paint one butterfly, use a straw to blow into the bubble solution. When bubbles have risen slightly above the rim, gently press a section of the butterfly on the bubbles. Repeat using different colors; then set the butterfly aside to dry. Next, bend a pipe cleaner in half and secure to the butterfly by twisting the pipe cleaner as shown. Curl the ends to resemble antennae. Display these beautiful "bubble-flies" for all to enjoy!

# A Book of Bubbles

Engage students in this booklet-making project and they will bubble over with excitement! To prepare, duplicate page 94 and the top portion of 95 to make a class supply. Gather the necessary supplies; then help each student follow the suggestions below to complete her pages. To bind each booklet, sequence the pages behind the cover and staple along the left-hand side. Send the completed booklets home for some good clean reading fun!

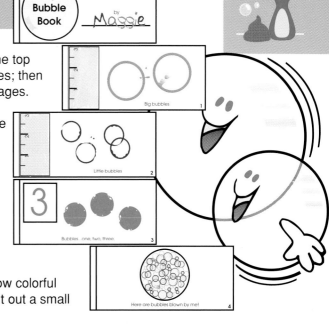

**Cover:** Print your name on the line. Color the bubble.
**Page 1:** Color the ruler. Make several bubble prints using paint and a juice can.
**Page 2:** Color the ruler. Make several bubble prints using paint and a film canister.
**Page 3:** Print the numeral 3 in the box. Make three bubble prints using paint and a small round sponge.
**Page 4:** Use the bubble paint solution from " 'Bubble-fly' Art" to blow colorful bubbles onto a half sheet of white paper. When the paint is dry, cut out a small circle. Glue your colorful bubble to the page.

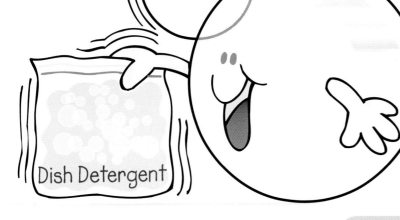

Shake, shake, shake
One, two, three
How many bubbles
Will we see?

# Shake It Up!

Use this simple experiment to show your little ones that some soaps make better bubbles! To prepare, have parents donate a bottle of baby shampoo and a bottle of dish detergent. Label two resealable plastic bags as shown. Gather your students and have each child predict which soap will produce more bubbles. Then add one cup of water and one-fourth teaspoon of each kind of soap into its labeled bag. Recite the rhyme above while each student takes a turn shaking the bags. After a few rounds of the rhyme, have students determine which soap worked best for making lots of tiny bubbles. Shake it up, baby!

## This Is Why
Dishwashing liquids contain more ingredients called *surfactants,* which produce bubbles. Baby shampoo contains only small amounts of surfactants.

# Behold: Bodacious Bubbles!

When your little ones experiment with different kinds of bubble blowers, a bounty of bubbles will result! In advance, put your favorite bubble solution in your water table; then gather a variety of bubble blowers (see the list at right). Have each child predict which bubble blower will make the smallest, largest, and most bubbles. Invite him to use different bubble blowers and then compare the results. Your water table is sure to be a "pop-ular" place!

**Bubble Blowers to Try:**
plastic cookie cutters
sunglasses without the lenses
wagon-wheel pasta or rigatoni
squares of plastic mesh produce bag
plastic funnels
mesh flyswatters
plastic drinking straws
plastic embroidery hoops
small and large plastic thread spools

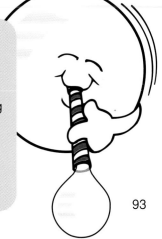

93

## Booklet Cover and Pages 1 and 2

Use with "A Book of Bubbles" on page 93.

My
Bubble
Book

by

_____

©2000 The Education Center, Inc. • *Science for All Seasons* • *Spring* • TEC3049

Big bubbles

**1**

Little bubbles

**2**

Bubbles...one, two, three.

**3**

Here are bubbles blown by me!

**4**

**Butterfly Pattern**
Use with "'Bubble-fly' Art" on page 92.

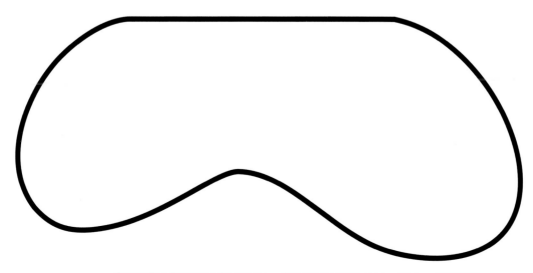

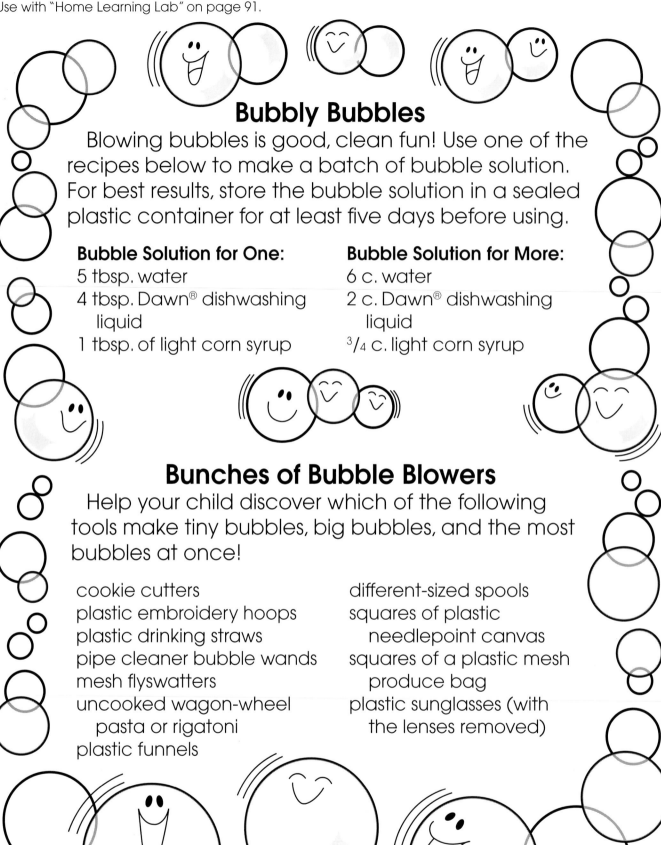

# Bubbly Bubbles

Blowing bubbles is good, clean fun! Use one of the recipes below to make a batch of bubble solution. For best results, store the bubble solution in a sealed plastic container for at least five days before using.

**Bubble Solution for One:**
5 tbsp. water
4 tbsp. Dawn® dishwashing liquid
1 tbsp. of light corn syrup

**Bubble Solution for More:**
6 c. water
2 c. Dawn® dishwashing liquid
$3/4$ c. light corn syrup

# Bunches of Bubble Blowers

Help your child discover which of the following tools make tiny bubbles, big bubbles, and the most bubbles at once!

cookie cutters
plastic embroidery hoops
plastic drinking straws
pipe cleaner bubble wands
mesh flyswatters
uncooked wagon-wheel
    pasta or rigatoni
plastic funnels

different-sized spools
squares of plastic
    needlepoint canvas
squares of a plastic mesh
    produce bag
plastic sunglasses (with
    the lenses removed)